DID JESUS DIE FOR *NOTHING?*

the evidence from Near Death Experiences

ORSON WEDGWOOD

Copyright © 2024 by Orson Wedgwood.

The right of Orson Wedgwood to be identified as the author of this work has been asserted. All rights reserved.

No part of this book may be reproduced, stored in a retrieval system, or transmitted, in any form, or by any means (electronic, mechanical, photocopying, recording or otherwise) without the prior written permission of the author, except in cases of brief quotations embodied in reviews or articles. It may not be edited, amended, lent, resold, hired out, distributed or otherwise circulated, without the publisher's written permission.

Permission can be obtained from www.orsonw.com

Published by Orson Wedgwood.

ISBN: 978-1-8383631-5-4

Cover design & interior formatting:
Mark Thomas / Coverness.com

TABLE OF CONTENTS

HELPFUL POINTERS 1

INTRODUCTION 3

CHAPTER 1: NDES, OBES AND RABBIT HOLES 11

CHAPTER 2: EARLY RESEARCH ON NDES 26

CHAPTER 3: SCIENTIFIC EVIDENCE FOR AND AGAINST NDES 35

CHAPTER 4: PROOF BEYOND REASONABLE DOUBT 64

CHAPTER 5: WHAT DO THE NDE RESULTS MEAN? 76

CHAPTER 6: WHAT ABOUT THE TEN PERCENT? 100

CHAPTER 7: WHICH RELIGION IS MOST CLOSELY ALIGNED TO WHAT NDES TELL US? 112

CHAPTER 8: UNDERSTANDING NDES IN THE LIGHT OF THE GOSPELS 135

CHAPTER 9: PASCAL'S WAGER—WITH A TWIST 167

APPENDIX: MEMORY WHEN THERE IS NO BRAIN 179

ENDNOTES 181

MY THANKS AND A SMALL REQUEST 185

BY THE SAME AUTHOR 187

ACKNOWLEDGEMENTS 189

ABOUT THE AUTHOR 191

HELPFUL POINTERS

All references indicated with a superscript number are found at the end of the book.

I write out acronyms the first time I use them in the text. But in case you forget any at a later point, you can return here:

- CA: cardiac arrest—the point at which the heart stops beating. It can also refer to the period after the heart has stopped beating; for example, while someone is in CA. It never refers to the period before the heart stops beating.
- CPR: cardiopulmonary resuscitation—manually pumping the heart and filling the lungs with air to try to induce ROSC.
- ECG: electrocardiograph or heart monitor.
- EEG: electroencephalogram—an electronic brain monitor.
- ER: Emergency Room
- HCPs: healthcare professionals. Doctors, nurses, and other medically trained experts involved in the first line delivery of healthcare.

- MRI: Magnetic Resonance Imaging – creates detailed images of structures in the body
- NDE: near death experience.
- NDEr: pronounced NDE-er— someone who had an NDE.
- OBE: out of body experience.
- PET: Positron Emission Tomography a form of scanning that uses chemical tracers to highlight structures in the body.
- ROSC: return of spontaneous circulation. This refers to the resumption of the heart beating and circulation of blood flow resuming. Use of the word "spontaneous" here refers to the fact that the heart can function without assistance from medical professionals.

Also, throughout this book the three words "consciousness," "soul," and "spirit" mean the same thing and are in effect interchangeable. They are the essence of what we call ourselves – our selfhood.

INTRODUCTION

This book will take you on a journey, one that has taken me decades to complete. You are lucky. This short read means you can perform the same journey in a few days! For me it was a journey of reasoning and faith that led to an understanding about our existence based on the information we have available to us from scientific near-death research, near death accounts, various religious teachings and specifically Christian Scripture.

My journey was delayed by getting stuck in the weeds of contradictory thinking. Some of this incomplete thinking is reflected in my previous book on this subject *NDE: Near Death Experiences and the AWARE Studies, Proof That the Soul and God Exist?* Now I have a clear position on the key issues raised by near death experiences (NDEs), one that is not only supported by evidence but is also aligned with the teachings of Jesus.

I have put that statement there to make it clear whom this book is for and whom it is not for. If you have no interest in Jesus, or you have a strong fixed universalist position; namely, that you are adamant that everyone goes to heaven and are offended by anything that challenges that position, then this book is not for you. However, if, like me, you are a believer who has been tempted by the allure of universalist claims made by some NDErs (those who have experienced NDEs), and yet cannot reconcile them with the stark warnings made by Jesus about a lost eternity, or you are someone who is genuinely curious as to how the teachings, life, and death of Jesus relate to what we have learned from NDEs, and are prepared to feel uncomfortable, then this book is most definitely for you.

NDEs have enthralled me and millions of others for over fifty years now. My interest was first sparked when I heard my father's NDE and was then amplified further when I began reading the many books on NDEs. I now run a blog for NDE nerds that looks at the scientific evidence for and against NDEs (awareofaware.com). Beyond the science I have found myself deeply moved with the countless stories of people who have traveled to what they call heaven, a place they describe as home, and where they meet dead relatives, "angelic" beings, and a supreme Being of Light whom they often refer to as God.

All the time that I absorbed myself in these incredible accounts of all kinds of people visiting heaven, I continued to attend Bible-believing churches which declared that only through Jesus could eternal life in heaven be guaranteed. This created a state of cognitive dissonance in me. On the one hand, having studied all the evidence for NDEs, specifically the evidence for the out of body experience (OBE) element of NDEs, as a rational scientist I could conclude only that they are real. And, by extrapolation, so therefore must be the claims that NDErs make. On the other hand, from the evidence I have from my walk with Jesus, from His teachings, and how I came to have my own life-changing transcendental experience of God, I could never in all conscience say everyone makes it to heaven.

So here is the question: How do you square the biblical understanding that eternal life is assured only through belief in Jesus with the universalist claims of so many NDErs, whose accounts appear genuine? The answer to that question in my case is twofold.

First, it required me as a scientist to do something that is normally anathema to me: to allow my confirmation bias, or faith as we Christians call it, to lead the way. That is less egregious from an intellectual perspective than it might at first seem, since there are genuinely conflicting and even contradictory pieces of evidence from NDE accounts. For instance, despite the claims of NDErs who say they have received their universalist view while conversing with "spirit guides" in heaven, there is in fact strong evidence from NDE research that a significant percentage go to a hellish place, and that possibly an even greater number may experience spiritual death, a theory I proposed in my previous book based on observations from respected research studies conducted by serious scientists. It is also consistent with my faith.

Given these inconsistencies and contradictory evidence, it meant that the only way to resolve this cognitive dissonance and form a final opinion on this vital subject would be to (1) choose a position first, in my case that Jesus was right, and (2) then select the evidence that supports that position. It is important to recognize that if I had decided I wanted to take the universalist position, it would also be possible to select favorable bits of evidence to support that position. NDEs do not give straightforward answers, and therefore force the individual to make a choice about worldviews.

Having done this, now more than ever I am convinced that the lack of "slam-dunk" evidence about the implications of NDEs with regard to faith or religion is in fact deliberate or designed. Put the tinfoil hat down! I do not mean that the human "establishment" is deliberately creating this situation, but rather that other "powers" may be at work. I believe we are supposed to have conflicting information, just as we are in this life. We are supposed to be making a choice. Having done that myself, while I cannot claim to show that my position is proven, I am intellectually comfortable with where I have landed and believe the balance of evidence and reasoned logic supports that position. That is the first "how;" namely, the chosen route I would take.

The second "how" is the information and reasoning that lead to the destination of my journey, and this book is designed to help others who also wish to answer this vital question in a rational manner. This last point is very important. In times past when the church has been challenged by new external information, it has often abandoned rational arguments and fallen back on strong declarations of faith that mean nothing to those who do not have faith in the first place, or whose faith is a bit wobbly. Yes, by allowing my so-called confirmation bias to lead the way when interpreting conflicting information, I am also taking a step of faith, but that is different from using faith to deny facts. My argument still makes sense and stands up to scrutiny when measured against the facts.

I believe that once NDEs are "scientifically" proven, as I am certain they will be, then Christianity will face both its greatest opportunity and greatest threat in centuries. My years of research and thinking on this subject have, for me at the very least, provided a path of reason through the universalist weeds that are the central part of this threat. Given that this is a path of reason, I am afraid you will need to engage your brain. I recommend reading this book over several days to allow your noodle to get to grips with some really deep stuff. While it is relatively short, the concepts the book explores and arguments I develop cannot be delivered in a Tweet or a TikTok video. I will try to avoid jargon and getting bogged down in too much science, but there is a certain level of knowledge you will need to gain to understand these arguments yourself and articulate them to others.

In the coming pages I will describe what NDEs are, why they are proven beyond doubt to be real through the one objectively testable core element of NDEs—the OBE. Then I will look at the other core elements people experience during an NDE. These are not objectively testable and given their variability can be regarded only as highly subjective, especially the many diverse accounts of heavenly realms and what meaning and lessons we can draw from these accounts regarding choice of faith. I will then look at the issues of hellish accounts and the possible reasons why so few older people have NDEs (spoiler alert it is not age-related memory changes). The latter provides very strong supporting evidence for the warnings of Jesus in the Gospels.

At this point I will gather together what core truths about the nature of our existence we can glean from all this new information from NDEs. Some leading proponents of NDEs believe these truths allow us to do away with religion (or form a new one based on the teachings of NDErs). Personally, I am not one for traditional "religion," which is often the following of prescribed arcane practices to achieve eternal life or a higher state of being. But I am one for active living faith that leads to connection with our creator. However, the inference of these NDE proponents, many of whom have swallowed the New Age philosophy in part or whole, is that not only can we do away with dusty irrelevant religion, but also faith in the teachings and example of any of the ancient prophets, including Jesus. They suggest that the ancient prophets might have glimpsed aspects of the truth, but NDEs provide us with the full picture.

In light of the new information and core truths NDEs from the past fifty years have provided humanity, I spend a significant section of the book seeing how the different major faiths measure up against the central understandings that arise from the accounts of NDErs. While I challenge the universalist claims of some NDE accounts, I do believe that the majority are sincere, and moreover that where their reports align identically, for example that our primary purpose is to love, we do indeed find eternal truths (although even on love the truth revealed by NDEs is incomplete, as I will discuss). The purpose of this exercise is to see if the claim that the newly revealed "truths" from NDEs transcend ancient teachings, as some claim, or whether some or all still stand firm.

Going through this process may offend some Christians, since surely it should be the other way around: "How do NDEs measure up to the teachings of Jesus?" Do not worry—that will come. I believe it is important to understand that if you take the central aligned learnings of NDErs to be truths, as most non-Christians will, even then it becomes clear that only Jesus, out of all the prophets, had a correct and complete understanding of the nature of our existence, of our eternal destiny, and of what God requires of us. The other religions all fall short—some more than others. For the "NDE curious" who do not have a Christian starting position, this is an extremely important point to establish.

Having shown that Jesus was the only "prophet" who got everything right, it is then time to look at the claims NDErs make that seem to contradict the teachings of Jesus. Here we learn that some things that may seem like contradictions, such as the issue of God's judgment, are not in fact contradictions. For some issues we do not have conclusive answers. However, on the core issue of universalism I have resolved the cognitive dissonance that troubled me for years by making a reasoned, but faith-based, choice about how I regard the claims of universalism. I hope my conclusions will give you a clear understanding of this topic and enable you to defend your mind from this appealing yet insidious line of thinking.

To give you a foretaste of where my thinking led, I did not allow faith to jettison reason out of my head. I do not subscribe to the idea promoted by some Christians that NDEs are entirely due to demonic interference (I do not completely discount this theory either). Neither do I find it satisfying to only treat NDEs that are biblically correct as being authentic and all others as made up or the result of demonic interference. I cannot subscribe to ideas or beliefs built on intellectual sand, and using confirmation bias, or faith, in such an extreme and crude way as a foundational position is quicksand—you will only ever preach to the converted and ill prepare them for a serious intellectual challenge from nonbelievers.

I am of the view that something subtler is going on, and the key is to treat all reports from NDEs as a whole, and authentic, despite their conflicting inferences. When you do that and are forced to ask the question as to why these contradictions exist, a conclusion consistent with my faith starts to emerge. The contradictions may arise partly from the result of subjective recollection or interpretation by NDErs, but I believe are more likely related to the importance of free will.

This last point was the "Aha!" moment for me and broke the impasse that had formed in my mind. Everything suddenly made sense. There is a lot to unpack when you view NDEs in this context, and this is the point that requires conformation bias, or that step of faith to make a choice, since I believe all NDE reports must be viewed in the context of the words of Jesus "No one has ever gone into heaven except the one who came from heaven— the Son of Man" (John 3:13). When you combine this with a core element of NDEs often referred to as "the point of no return," all NDEs can be viewed in a different light from how they are currently by the mainstream media, the NDE community, and even some Christians. No NDEr has ever entered God's heaven

On the other hand, while I am now certain that universalism is an insidious lie, I do not believe the evidence—either from NDEs or Jesus' teachings— points to Christian exceptionalism. Some who call themselves Christians go to hell, and some who never encountered Christ in this life may go to heaven. I show how the learnings from NDEs and the teachings of Jesus align on this. I know there are Christians who will claim this is heresy, but I will show why I believe it is not, using Christ's words.

Then I answer the question posed on the cover of this book: Did Jesus die for nothing? Having slain the lie that NDEs prove universalism to be true, a lie propagated sincerely by many NDE proponents, particularly New Agers, but even some Christians, this becomes a very simple question to answer. While I do not completely understand the mechanics of how Jesus paid our ransom, I accept it as truth and without it my eternity is lost. But there is an even more fundamentally important aspect of Christ's death on the cross that means it was central and vital to everything—His physical resurrection.

The meaning and importance of this event, when viewed in light of learnings from science and NDEs, is everything. It confirms beyond any doubt who He really was, which makes His warnings in the Gospels even more prescient.

At the end of the journey we discuss the new post-materialistic choice that faces humanity in light of recent information NDEs have provided us. Given that NDEs prove beyond reasonable doubt that the soul is able to survive the death of the body, I believe the eternal destiny of the soul comes down to choosing between (1) the NDE inspired teachings on universalism or (2) believing the teachings of Jesus, which include many warnings of hell and destruction for the majority of souls, a choice akin to Pascal's wager—but with a twist.

Let us prepare for the start of the journey. It is time to delve into the science of NDEs.

CHAPTER 1: NDES, OBES AND RABBIT HOLES

Morgan Freeman: "Is there any scientific support for the idea of the soul?"

Dr. Sam Parnia: "Today we call the soul consciousness in science. So, we can test this theory scientifically and see—does consciousness continue or does it stop? The evidence we have is that when a person dies . . . the soul—the consciousness—doesn't become annihilated . . . at least in the early period of death."[1]

Above is an excerpt from an interview Morgan Freeman conducted with Dr. Sam Parnia, MD, in New York as part of Freeman's 2016 TV series called The Story of God.

Just contemplate for a moment the significance of this leading physician and research scientist's words: when a person's body dies, the soul survives. Given their source, these words turn the modern materialistic world upside down and they are what NDE research is all about. This leads to an obvious question: If Dr. Parnia and many other leading physicians and scientists are saying that the evidence supports the understanding that the soul survives death, why is this not the accepted view of the wider academic establishment?

The reason for this is that to date none of the studies that research the phenomenon of NDEs has provided *scientific proof* that the consciousness can survive without a functioning brain.

Scientific proof is a specific expression that refers to overwhelming evidence obtained using the scientific method of hypothesis generation and experimentation. Until we have evidence from predetermined experiments in a controlled study, we do not have scientific proof. Without this the academic establishment will cling like a barnacle on a sinking ship to its default materialist position; namely, that all phenomena have a natural cause.

Dr. Parnia uses the word "evidence" in relation to science, not "proof." It is an important distinction. I will shortly summarize the scientific evidence for and against NDEs (there is much more detail on this in my book *NDE: Near Death Experiences and the AWARE Studies, Proof That the Soul and God Exist?*). But I agree that we do not yet have scientific proof that NDEs are real.

So why do I say in the introduction that NDEs are proven real beyond reasonable doubt?

Because they are!

Are you confused? Read on. All will become clear and you will see in the next couple of chapters why the materialist ship has been wrecked on the rock of reason, even if absolute scientific proof is, for the moment, lacking.

To understand why the available evidence proves beyond reasonable doubt that NDEs are real, we need to understand what NDEs are.

NDES: NEAR DEATH, DURING DEATH, AFTER DEATH, NEVER DEAD?

The term "near death experience" suggests an experience when someone is near death or appears to actually be dead. However, there is a lot of debate among scientists and clinicians about exactly when NDEs occur. Some believe it happens while a person is clinically dead; others think it occurs before clinical death, or during the few seconds after cardiac arrest (CA) when the heart has stopped and the brain is in the process of shutting down, others when the brain starts up again after 'return of spontaneous circulation' - ROSC.

In his book *The Lazarus Effect*, Dr. Parnia refers to NDEs as "actual death experiences." In a recent paper he published along with other HCPs and researchers, he amended this further to "recorded experiences of death."[2] I will not use the acronyms for these as I will not use the terms again as everyone understands them as NDEs, but he argues that the term "near death" is misleading, since, according to medical criteria, those who experience NDEs are clinically dead, not near death. They then return to life from clinical death once they are revived (achieve ROSC). I understand what he is getting at, but I think he is wrong for reasons I will get into later. However, it brings us to an important question: What is death?

Death is regarded by most people as the end of everything and is not a popular topic of conversation. It is rarely a pleasant experience, maybe involving long battles against painful diseases or, in extreme cases, the sound of a gunshot or seeing a sharp blade slicing through the air towards one.

Despite the obvious unpleasantness of the events immediately preceding death, I think most who fear death do so more because of the questions about what happens afterwards. The uncertainty and fear caused by those who lack faith gives rise to very real anxiety. Many people who read my blog contact me saying how anxious they are about death, and seek reassurance that NDEs prove that our souls do not die. I am careful about the responses I provide.

So, from an emotional human perspective death is for many a terminal event to existence on this planet with uncertain consequences to their consciousness (soul), causing them fear. But what about from a scientific perspective? Things get a bit more complicated here—do they not always?

Death is arguably the absence of life.

What is life or, more specifically, what constitutes a living human being?

To be alive, your blood must be circulating at sufficient levels to provide oxygenated blood to your vital organs and, at the same time, remove blood containing waste products such as carbon dioxide, which is exhaled, or toxins filtered by your kidneys and excreted in your urine, or metabolized by the liver. Once blood flow falls below critical levels, organs stop functioning, toxic substances start accumulating, and the cells that constitute your body are eventually damaged beyond repair. Especially relevant to this book is the fact that within seconds of stopped blood flow, the brain is no longer capable of conscious activity. In fact, once your heart beats below around 35 beats per minute, your brain is rarely able to sustain consciousness. People who suffer from bradycardia, an irregular and often slow heartbeat, often experience syncope, or fainting.

Consciousness as scientifically defined—thought, self-awareness, observations, and so on—is a higher function of the brain demanding large amounts of chemical energy and oxygen to sustain. In fact, the brain is the most power-hungry organ in the body, using more energy than any other.

When processes involving consciousness occur, there is a lot of activity on what is called an electroencephalogram—an electronic brain monitor—or EEG. The same is true of dreams, which are just a different state of consciousness. In either instance, for such consciousness to occur, the brain and heart need to function at normal or near normal levels. To be alive, and stay alive, your heart needs to be pumping blood.

The standard, or legal, definition of the word "death" is the irreversible state in which a person has no heartbeat or conscious activity. Note the use of the word irreversible. Death is normally defined as a permanent state. *Clinical death* is the one exception to this rule. It is a state where again there is no heartbeat or brain activity, but the person could still recover either spontaneously or through medical intervention, or they could progress to permanent death. In the absence of specialist equipment, either form of death is determined by the lack of a pulse and the pupil's lack of response to light. When the equipment is available, it is when both the ECG (electrocardiograph or heart monitor) and the EEG are flatlining.

Before the advent of modern resuscitation techniques in the 1950s, most people who had a cardiac arrest (CA) were indeed "dead." But sometimes a person who appeared dead would come back to life; which is why in Victorian times, people were sometimes buried with a bell in their coffin so they could ring it and be "saved by the bell." However, it is unlikely their hearts had stopped and then restarted unaided. It is more likely they entered some sort of "death-like" coma with minimal respiration or detectable heartbeat.

Although Dr. Parnia and other ER healthcare professionals prefer to define death as the cessation of heart and brain activity, they also acknowledge that there is a difference between this clinical definition of immediate death—which is reversible if ROSC occurs very soon afterwards—and irreversible or permanent death, which, in the absence of major organ damage, can be a process that takes hours or more to complete.

Cellular death is the key factor in permanent death. Once a certain number of cells have died, it is no longer possible to bring a viable body back to life. This point was once usually considered to be a few minutes after the heart and brain had stopped functioning. Now, through modern resuscitation techniques, which keep blood pumping around the body and oxygen flowing into the lungs, the point at which permanent death occurs can be delayed for much longer than the 5 minutes previously thought to be the limit. In fact, blood flow may not even be necessary to preserve cells for at least the first hours after death.

A groundbreaking but notorious piece of research published in April 2019 shows the potential viability of cells in pig brains taken from an abattoir hours after the pigs had been slaughtered.[3] This points to the possibility of people being revived hours or more after death with much of their brain tissue remaining undamaged. Current thinking in the field has moved to an understanding that brain damage is not necessarily caused by cellular decay in the hours immediately after death, but by reperfusion injury on ROSC. This injury is caused by the deoxygenated blood (deoxygenated because the brain had used all the oxygen in it) that had lingered in the brain being suddenly replaced by fully oxygenated blood. To avoid this, techniques are being developed to gradually reintroduce different fluids to allow a slower transition that causes less or no damage.

Another way of preserving and protecting a body during clinical death is by lowering its temperature. Indeed, there have been several instances where people have fallen into extremely cold water and, after being clinically dead for 10 minutes or longer, they were resuscitated and staged a full recovery. A well-known example of this is when a boat capsized in a lake in Denmark in 2011, and seven children were thrown into the icy water.[4] All of them were clinically dead with no heartbeat for 6 hours, but through careful, slow warming, all seven eventually achieved ROSC with no permanent brain damage. Another well-documented example is of Anna Bågenholm, who in 2000, fell through a frozen lake and remained under water for 40 minutes before her body was recovered.[5] After receiving resuscitation, she too eventually achieved ROSC. Anna was clinically dead with no heartbeat or blood flow to the brain, but due to the sudden cooling of the body, the process of cellular decay was slowed, which allowed a viable recovery. She was dead but not permanently dead.

This concept of cooling the body to avoid cellular damage is used in certain types of surgery—on the brain, the heart, or on the vascular system—when flowing blood would make operating impossible. Hypothermic circulatory arrest is achieved by artificially cooling the body slowly and stopping the heart. Surgeons then try to perform surgery within an hour, restart the heart, and slowly warm the body back up. During this time patients are clinically dead, but the technique is now so reliable that it is routinely performed around the world in major hospitals. Not surprisingly, NDEs have been reported by some of the patients undergoing this procedure—which I will discuss later.

In summary, there is both clinical and permanent death. Most NDEs reported obviously occurred during clinical death—it is tough to report anything if you are permanently dead! (Although, bizarrely, this point is lost on some materialist researchers, as you will find out in the coming pages.) I say most reported NDEs because some OBEs occurred while the patient was in a coma after the initial period of clinical death. In the vast majority of NDEs the NDEr was clinically dead at some point.

Skeptical scientists and physicians who do not believe the validity of NDEs or that the consciousness is a separate entity able to survive death, argue that any person who can be revived after CA has the potential for consciousness or some level of brain function between the time the heart stops and ROSC. The argument they promote is that the brain is still functional; therefore it could have functioned.

In general, this is shown not to be the case by the universal observation that consciousness is associated with strong and distinct EEG activity. The fact is that when the heart stops beating, noteworthy EEG activity of this kind stops within a few seconds. Believing that a brain can produce consciousness when there is no supply of oxygenated blood is like believing a computer without a source of power can perform the function of processing.

Both are impossible. A brain without blood supply may stay functional for a period, but without blood flow, it cannot function.

The only exceptions of consciousness in the absence of a heartbeat in humans are when an artificial supply of oxygenated blood is provided at sufficiently high levels to allow higher-level brain function. There have been rare instances when advanced CPR has been administered and the patient has had passing conscious episodes despite having no pulse.[6] This is due to the high quality of the resuscitation being administered, which produces sufficient blood flow to allow the brain to function at near normal levels. There is one particularly harrowing account of a man who stayed fully conscious after his CA during CPR, but the HCPs were unable to restore spontaneous circulation and had to make the decision to let him die while he was still conscious. What a horrible moment for all.

While reports of momentary consciousness during CPR in the absence of a heartbeat are very rare, they do provide skeptics with a potentially plausible explanation as to why people may have conscious episodes and form memories such as those described in NDEs. However, even if that explanation were true for some elements of an NDE, it does not and cannot explain validated out of body experiences (OBEs).

OBES: INDISPUTABLE OBJECTIVE EVIDENCE AND SUGAR CUBES

I will get into more detail later but, suffice to say, there is no natural explanation, whether it be drugs, undetected brain activity during CPR, or any other physiological phenomenon, that can account for a fully validated OBE. This central fact lies at the heart of the first part of this book. If validated OBEs exist, we have proof that consciousness is a separate entity from the brain, that it can survive death, and therefore materialism is sunk. It also raises questions about physical resurrection for those who die before Jesus' return.

I ask my fellow believers who hold fast to the understanding that everyone is physically resurrected on the day of judgment, to first "car park" those concerns as I will briefly discuss them once we have established what the evidence for OBEs is. Second, I ask them to accept that physical resurrection should not be a "make or break" article of faith, and that many Bible believing Christians who, while believing that Jesus was physically resurrected, do not believe their own earthly bodies will be resurrected, but that rather they will inhabit new, heavenly bodies which are similar but superior. If you believe those people are condemned for holding this understanding, then this book really is not for you. But if you can accept that it is a topic of theological debate that does not alter the eternal destiny of a Christian whichever side they take, then read on. I will discuss this and provide an alternative to the dualist understanding that arises if you accept OBEs to be real. Also, whenever I refer to dualism in this book, I am speaking of Platonic dualism—the belief that the soul inhabits the body, and the two are separate but joined together in this body. Let us see what the evidence says.

Thousands of patients over the years claim to have experienced consciousness in the form of OBEs while their hearts and brains were not functioning. These people sometimes describe visual and/or auditory recollections of events occurring around them, or people near them, or even names of medications used—all details they could not have been aware of if they were truly unconscious. In about 25% of NDEs, NDErs reported making these observations from outside of their bodies; hence the term "out of body experience" or OBE.

As mentioned, many NDErs are credible citizens, as are the doctors and healthcare workers who recorded their testimonials. Many doctors and nurses in ER rooms have their own set of NDE stories that defy natural explanation. This was in fact how Sam Parnia came to be interested in the subject.

I also became interested after two people described NDEs with OBEs to me. One was a woman I briefly dated who told me how she had an asthma attack while hiking in Peru. She popped out of her body and saw her friends try to resuscitate her. She also saw two of her friends kiss outside of the tent her body was in, something that was later verified. The other NDE I heard of was experienced by someone closer to me—my father. When he was a young boy he was cycling and got knocked down by a car. Suddenly he found himself hovering above his body while people tried to revive him—a classic example of an OBE. There is one thing I am certain of: my father did not lie.

An OBE is one of the core elements of an NDE, and since it is the only piece of evidence we can test objectively, it is the only evidence that can be validated. This can be achieved through reliable third-party human confirmation of the NDEr's observations or by using the scientific method. I will show that OBEs during NDEs have been proven real beyond any reasonable doubt using the first method a bit later. However, scientifically proving that an OBE is real, while illusive for logistical reasons, would prove to the stubborn academic establishment that NDEs are real too. By extrapolation this would prove scientifically that the soul is able to survive death as an entity separate from the body. A scientifically proven OBE is to academic materialism as the iceberg was to the Titanic.

The answer may seem obvious, but it is important to ask the question "Why would a validated OBE establish that the soul lives beyond death?"

If the brain and heart have stopped working, the eyes are closed, and the visual and auditory nerves are inactive—it is impossible for the brain to observe or record visual or auditory stimuli. There is no natural scientific explanation for how they could physically observe or record anything. If reports of OBEs during NDEs are verified, there is only one viable explanation: the consciousness is operating and making observations independently of the body after the body's death. Thus the consciousness is a separate entity able to survive without the body.

While this answer may be obvious, it is far from simple once we grasp the philosophical implications.

We will now briefly go down a rabbit hole for the next page or two. If grappling with a bit of philosophy is not why you bought this book, skip this and pick things up below in the section "Exiting the rabbit hole." It would be better if you did not, though. You may need a bit of patience and have to stop, reread, and think about what the evidence is telling us. Remember, I have had this stuff rattling round my brain for 20 years or more, so if the idea that our existence is not what we understand as "real" is entirely new to you, it may be a bit discombobulating.

ENTERING THE RABBIT HOLE

How this consciousness can "see" without the use of eyes or "hear" without the use of ears is a conundrum that raises fundamental philosophical questions about the nature of how we observe the universe and what the observable universe actually is.

While questioning whether or not what we see and hear is "real" may be unsettling, it is an obvious question that arises from this central paradox lying at the heart of the OBE phenomena. In fact, many NDErs, if not all, come back and say this is not real life—the other side is real. In this light, I feel it is worth getting some kind of handle on this before we go further so as to avoid any sense of inconsistency in the conclusions that can be drawn about the evidence OBEs provide.

From a materialist scientific understanding, consciousness needs the brain to hear—this process is well understood. Sensors in our ears pick up sound waves that are translated into electrical signals, which are sent along nerves that lead to our brain. These electrical signals are then translated into signals our consciousness hears as sound. Hearing is so automatic and intuitive that we do not think about how it occurs. We just hear. We are unaware of the fact that our consciousness hears nothing without the brain interpreting electronic nerve signals as sounds.

This leads to an obvious question. If consciousness survives death, and in life it needs the brain to hear, how can it hear, or sense anything, once the brain is dead or inactive?

This is the paradox at the center of the whole NDE/OBE phenomenon. By citing that the brain is inactive—therefore incapable of hearing or seeing—we are ignoring the apparent need of the consciousness to have a functioning brain to hear, see, and record a memory of what is seen and heard!

It is a mind-bending paradox, but that fact does not invalidate the veracity of NDEs or OBEs; it just demands explanations about the nature of existence that lie beyond materialistic understanding and that we are unable to prove.

If OBEs are real, it must be true that the consciousness, once free of the body, is able to observe our familiar physical world without the need for the physical equipment it normally uses to experience physical reality while alive. In other words, when we are physically alive our consciousness experiences the physical world using physical equipment in our bodies, but once we are physically dead, the same consciousness is still able to observe the physical world, but without the use of physical equipment. In one state we are physical participants; in the other, just conscious observers.

That can be the only explanation for how people see and hear validated events in our world while clinically dead during OBEs.

This raises numerous questions about the physical world, and the answers can only be theoretical and philosophical in nature. They are completely untestable outside obscure mathematics but, at the same time, they lead us to ponder the nature of the experienced physical "reality" we are accustomed to. It is a question related to the meaning of life.

If you think this is all crazy, just think about dreams. In dreams we see and hear things as though they are real, but they never happened in our physical reality. Our consciousness hears sounds that were never transmitted via auditory nerves and sees sights that were never transmitted along optical nerves. It experiences things as though they are real even though they do not physically happen.

When it comes to the nature of the physical universe, other than hints from the field of quantum mechanics, theories that the universe is not even a physical construct as we perceive it to be are a matter of speculation. But given Christians are told that all we see around us is the result of a creative mind of vast genius, who are we to say in what manner it exists? After all, the actual physical space the entire human population takes up when squished together and all the gaps between subatomic particles are removed is about the same size as a sugar cube! (Do a web search if you do not believe me.)

Theoretical physicists who have devoted their considerable intellect to grappling with the mathematics of space, matter, and time are capable of understanding and explaining our existence at a quantum level by using the implications of wave particle duality to subatomic particles and their components. But their theories, which are often revised or disproved with time, provide mere hints about how everything we understand to be real came into being and is sustained.

By the way, for those into their philosophy, I am not a proponent of philosophical idealism, which some argue NDEs prove. Nor am I convinced that the world in which we live is the "true reality." To me it seems like some sort of construct designed for a very specific purpose that NDEs hint at and Jesus clearly refers to, albeit through parables. More on that later, but I believe that even if this created world in which we find ourselves is not "real," our actions, experience, thoughts, and intentions to others and to events in this created world are very real. They are what matter. I believe that our souls are real even if they are currently existing within a "test environment." This may feel anathema to some Christians, but I am of the view that it is entirely consistent with what the first books of Genesis and Jesus reveal to us.

Another mind bender is how memory of these experiences gets recorded in the brain without the brain functioning. That will be discussed in the Appendix, but the clue lies in the question "Is memory even recorded in the brain?" Very strong evidence that it is not emerges from NDE research.

For now, if it is proven that consciousness is able to survive independently of the brain and body, then the paradox of seeing without eyes and hearing without ears, and all the questions that raises, while unsettling, is also proven true.

EXITING THE RABBIT HOLE

To proceed without getting any more bogged down, we must accept that OBEs can be explained only by allowing for a consciousness that has the potential to observe and record memories of events while independent of the body and brain.

Dr. Parnia has previously asserted that according to scientific evidence, for at least a short time after death, the soul, or consciousness, is indeed able to persist without the "host" body. This is hugely controversial to a scientific community that works under the informal dogma of methodological materialism—meaning there is always a natural explanation for everything. As a result, there is powerful opposition from the academic establishment to formal research into NDEs.

Since the emergence of the theory of evolution, which cemented the modern foundation of science in materialism, many scientists have assumed that consciousness is something produced by the brain. No one has ever been able to explain how, but it is postulated that our sense of being—our ability to interpret our senses and communicate with the world around us—is a result of the brain's activity. The understanding that NDEs, and specifically OBEs, are evidence that the consciousness can exist independently of a functioning brain contradicts this materialistic understanding. Specifically, it points to the brain and the rest of our body as being just a "host" or "receptacle" of our consciousness or soul, rather than the generator of it.

It is widely understood that the scientific community is disproportionately represented by atheists compared to those from other disciplines. Moreover, those who do have faith are wary about speaking out about their beliefs since doing so can have career-limiting effects. In an email I received from Dr. Parnia, he alluded to the significant opposition he had experienced in setting up his studies. He also says as much in his book Lucid Dying published in August 2024:

> Another major challenge was that then, as now, most doctors and scientists wouldn't go near this subject. It was and still remains somewhat of a taboo subject. I had to think carefully about the possible effects on my career. I was a young doctor just starting out and I didn't want this to possibly end my career, before I had even started it properly.

Scientists, like all humans, are tribal. The scientific tribe has become one of the most powerful tribes on earth as it holds the keys to knowledge that is central to modern living. Because many members of this tribe have publicly adopted an atheist stance and built their credibility around this position, they feel threatened when challenged with evidence that undermines their central materialistic belief. When people are threatened, they do not always respond fairly or even rationally, and such has been the case with some scientists in their treatment of any viable research that does not support their materialistic atheist position.

If the OBE was proven to be real, it would provide evidence consistent with religious belief and completely shatter the current central dogma of science—materialism—that has been in place since the 1800s.

While the stubborn barnacle of establishment thinking still clings to the sinking ship of materialism, demanding scientific verification before it abandons its dying and damaging philosophy, I am certain we already have proof beyond reasonable doubt that OBEs during NDEs are real.

Let us see if you agree.

CHAPTER 2: EARLY RESEARCH ON NDES

THE FOUNDING OF THE FIELD: PRE-1980

Now we can really start out on the journey, and will be walking in the footsteps of the pioneers of the field.

NDEs have reportedly occurred throughout history, even going back to antiquity. The first medical report was by a French military doctor in 1740. However, before the advent of modern CPR in the 1950s, spontaneous revival was not common. If you had a heart attack and your heart stopped, you were considered permanently dead, and the opportunity to experience an NDE was extremely limited. As a result, reports of NDEs were rare, and NDEs were not fully understood for what they were: that someone had actually died and come back to life. In our modern era, people dying and being revived with CPR happens every day in many of the hundreds of thousands of hospitals across the world. If the NDE is a real phenomenon, one would expect to hear about them occurring more frequently throughout the past six decades—and this is precisely what has happened, especially in North America and Europe.

Initially, however, such patient reports were dismissed by physicians and nurses as hallucinations, or even as evidence of psychiatric disorders. Given the skeptical response from health professionals in industrialized countries, many of the early NDErs kept quiet about their experiences, only disclosing them when the public, and some in the medical profession, became more accepting. The perception of NDEs began changing after the 1975 publication of Raymond Moody's book *Life After Life*. Moody, a clinical psychologist who had listened to patients' reports about NDEs for a number of years, decided that the phenomenon was most likely real. His book, which recounted many of the experiences, caused a media storm, and interest has only grown since.

There were a number of subsequent books by other leaders in the field, such as psychologist Ken Ring, who published *Life at Death* in 1980, and Dr. Michael Sabom, who published *Recollections of Death: A Medical Investigation* in 1984. A cardiologist and professor of medicine, Dr. Sabom was the first physician to publish on this topic, bringing it even more attention. Bruce Greyson was another founding father of research into NDEs, and in 1984 co-authored the book *The Near Death Experience: Problems, Prospects, Perspectives*.

This initial flurry of activity was followed by years of more books of subjective accounts confirmed by healthcare professionals. Some included OBE reports in which patients reported seeing objects in neighbouring rooms and even on ledges outside the hospital while clinically dead—reports that were later verified independently.

One of the more famous NDEs that has been discussed over the years is that of Pam Reynolds, a well-known record producer in the 1980s and 1990s. She had a brain aneurysm in 1991 and was deliberately brought into a state of near death using deep hypothermic circulatory arrest (cooling the body and stopping the heart)—so doctors could operate and stop the leaking in her brain. During the operation, she had ear buds taped into her ears that played a very loud sound so the doctors could record any EEG activity and know when to increase sedation.

Pam Reynolds described "popping" outside of her head. For a while she said she remained in the room, hovering above her body. She observed the number of people in the room, the instruments being used, and a discussion around which artery to use for a procedure. She also reported meeting a dead relative and then being pushed back into her broken body. After the operation, she told the neurosurgeon what she had seen, and he confirmed all the details. He was as convinced as she was that she had had an NDE with an OBE since he believed it was impossible for her to have seen or heard anything naturally. This is a typical "anecdotal" account, albeit reported by a well-known figure and verified by a respected medical professional.

The details of the common core elements of NDEs started to become better characterized and eventually formalized in the Greyson NDE scale, which I will discuss in more detail in chapter 3 below. Books and TV shows sensationalizing NDEs were all the rage in the 1980s and early 1990s. But as time went by, the reluctance of the medical and academic establishment to give it serious thought, and the endless insistence of materialist scientists that NDEs were produced by the brain, meant that those who believed in NDEs were categorized with those who believe in astrology. Thousands of reports by credible witnesses, including pilots, lawyers, engineers, servicemen, teachers, and university professors, along with verifications from reliable attending medical professionals, meant absolutely nothing to the hardened skeptics who control the narrative.

However, not all the blame for disbelief lies with materialist skeptics—the NDE community itself must also be blamed. Dozens of NDE websites and societies, some of which were once balanced and reliable, began to embrace the excesses of the New Age movement and espouse concepts alien to Western thinking, and they were eventually regarded as somewhat bizarre. Some of these New Age inferences are also not necessarily correlated with the NDE reports of the early researchers. Proponents of the New Age movement might explain that this is because the vast majority of early work was conducted in the West, and mostly in the USA, which is predominantly Christian. Either way, it is fair to say that the NDE community has attracted more than its fair share of unhinged attention seekers. As well, many of these websites encourage people to add their own NDEs, and while this may attract a large number of genuine reports, any such accounts leave them open to the obvious accusation of not being remotely objective, or of describing experiences that fall outside of the classical definition of an NDE.

For scientists like me and others, this is very off-putting and gives plenty of ammunition to the materialist skeptics. Thankfully, some serious and highly qualified medical researchers, who shared a genuine curiosity about the subject, in the late 1980s began to conduct more rigorous academic clinical research.

At this point on our journey the road becomes a little bit steeper for a while as we navigate a summary of important clinical and scientific data that underpins our understanding of NDEs (for a detailed account read my previous book *Near Death Experiences and the AWARE Studies, Proof That the Soul and God Exist?*, which I update yearly as new data emerges, or my blog awareofaware.com, which I try to update live). Stick with the next few pages and Chapter 3, as I believe the rewards will be worth your effort.

To be able to really understand and articulate why NDEs are proven real and the implications this has, you need to build your position on the solid foundation of reliable information gathered by respected academics rather than just the subjective accounts from individuals published in books or presented on YouTube. The latter are a lot more exciting, and I promise we will come to a remarkable selection of those shortly, but we need to ground these accounts in research that has substance.

This is precisely what the researchers themselves realized, and that anecdotal accounts, even ones as convincing as Pam Reynolds's, were not going to be enough to persuade the skeptics. So, these researchers set about designing studies that would investigate the phenomenon by using the scientific method. This consists of systematic observation, measurement, and experiment, alongside the formulation, testing, and modification of hypotheses.

A hypothesis is a supposition or proposed explanation made on the basis of limited evidence as a starting point for further investigation. Simply put, a hypothesis is a statement that potentially explains an observed phenomenon and the scientific method is the process by which the statement is determined true or not. It is important to note that a hypothesis can never be proven—it can only be disproven. While a statement might be proven true, it is possible that another statement might also be proven true, which would create a competing hypothesis. Let us think of an example from history:

Observation: the sun rises in the east and sets in the west.
Hypothesis: the sun is going around the earth.

For millennia that hypothesis was accepted as fact, until new observations disproved it. I will come back to this later.

If enough experiments provide overwhelming evidence supporting a hypothesis and none have disproven it, then it will likely be accepted and become theory. Now, having said that hypotheses cannot be proven, for the sake of simplicity, I am going to be naughty and use the word "validate" in this text. For the sake of the pedants I will put it in quotes. The scientific method is crudely summarized as follows.

Make observations > generate a hypothesis that explains those observations > design and conduct an experiment that tests the hypothesis > evidence provides support for hypothesis > hypothesis is "validated" and becomes theory > end process—or experiments show false/imperfect findings > modify original hypothesis or generate new one > design new experiment, and so on.

This is the way good science is conducted, and I will come back to this later a number of times because, unfortunately, good scientific practice has not always been deployed in the field of NDE research.

PUBLISHED SCIENTIFIC STUDIES: 1980S AND ONWARD

In my world, you are not taken seriously as a researcher unless you are published in a reputable scientific journal. The world's two most respected general medical journals are *The Lancet* and *The New England Journal of Medicine*. Often, to be published in a journal such as these, you must produce research that either generates advances in knowledge about a disease or phenomenon, sometimes enabling a hypothesis to be made on causality and treatment, or research that either "validates" or disproves a hypothesis.

For NDEs to be considered a subject of genuine scientific enquiry rather than just an eccentric belief in a paranormal phenomenon, medical researchers needed to initially undertake well-designed research studies that observed and characterized these experiences in a more scientific manner. Having done this, they would need to devise further studies to either "validate" or disprove any hypothesis arising from the initial observational studies. There is a hypothesis around OBEs and NDEs that I will mention a bit later, and studies have been done and are ongoing that may "validate" this hypothesis, but things have not gone as well as might have been hoped. To understand why, we need to look at how the studies were designed and identify any potential shortcomings.

What is the nature of a research study? For this book we will look at two types that feed into the scientific method (observation > hypothesis > experiment). The first is purely observational and gathers information on a condition to advance understanding; the second one tests a hypothesis of causality or of treatment, usually arising from the information gathered in the first type of study. In a well-designed research study looking to "validate" or disprove a hypothesis, an experiment is then created.

Let us take an example I have worked on in my career, which is about to revolutionize Alzheimer's disease (AD) treatment. This is a bit of a detour, but given the prevalence of AD, one I hope you will find interesting and maybe even of personal relevance (my father died at a relatively young age of AD, so I am acutely aware of the devastation it causes).

Observation: Early studies on people with dementia due to AD showed that they had higher amounts of what are known as Beta Amyloid plaques in the brain postmortem than people who never developed dementia.

Hypothesis: the "Beta Amyloid hypothesis;" namely, that higher amounts of the protein Beta Amyloid were the primary cause of AD and that reducing these amounts would reduce the likelihood of developing dementia. Beta Amyloid therefore became the primary target for many pharmaceutical and biotech companies in drug development for AD.

Experiment: A biotech company creates a drug that shows promise in a lab and in animal models at removing Beta Amyloid from the brain. After assessing the safety of the drug, they will test the hypothesis—that a drug which removes Beta Amyloid from the brain will reduce rates of dementia—in an experiment or study on humans. They take a group of patients with high levels of Beta Amyloid in the brain, but who have not yet developed full-blown dementia, split them in two, giving one half the drug and the other a placebo (a tablet, or fluid, that looks like the drug but does not contain any active substance).

A very important part of designing the study, and one that is vital when it comes to discussing the current set of results from NDE studies, is the issue of "powering" the study. "Powering" a study is ensuring there are enough patients in the study to create an observable and statistically meaningful effect. A statistician makes this calculation using data from previous proof-of-concept studies that give a ballpark figure of effect, and including enough subjects in the new study to ensure a high level of confidence that the effect is real.

Well-designed studies follow a number of principles:

- Patients are "randomized." This occurs when a computer randomly assigns study patients to go on either the drug or the placebo, thereby removing physician bias.
- The trial should also be double blinded—neither the patient nor the healthcare professional involved knows whether the patient is taking the drug or the placebo.
- A good clinical study is "prospective" in that it is set up before patients are recruited, and patients are included before any "event" has occurred, such as, for example, taking a drug or placebo (or having a CA), to ensure consistency in terms of the data collected, the types of patients admitted to the study, and the degree of randomization and blinding. Retrospective studies that select patients after the events occurred are much more open to bias and irregularities. (The books on NDEs by Moody, Greyson, Sabom and others, were all based on retrospective anecdotal accounts.)

In terms of Alzheimer's, once the study has been set up using these principles, the study investigators, usually clinicians who work in public healthcare, follow these patients over a suitable period of time to determine if there is a difference in the rate of onset or worsening of dementia symptoms between the two groups. If the group taking the drug shows a slower rate or even a halting of decline in cognition compared to the placebo, then the biotech's statement in relation to the hypothesis about the drug is validated.

The amazing news is that, after decades of failure, a number of recent studies have shown that the Beta Amyloid targeting hypothesis—that a drug targeting the Beta Amyloid protein can slow the progression of AD—is strongly supported by the evidence. While effects observed were modest, showing a slowing in decline of about 25–30%, there were signals that if used really early on in the disease process, the effects may be much more significant. Being an optimist, I believe we will be able to completely stop the disease in the not-too-distant future. Diagnosing AD early and offering treatment before one even sees symptoms is set to become one of the biggest and most controversial topics of conversation in healthcare over the coming decade.

If you did not know this before, hopefully you now have a better idea of the process behind research using the scientific method. This will help us to build a picture of how scientific research in the field of NDEs has progressed, why it has stalled, and why, even despite this recent stalling, we have proof beyond reasonable doubt that the consciousness leaves the body—thus supporting the hypothesis I propose in relation to this.

Let us first briefly examine the scientific evidence relating to NDEs.

CHAPTER 3: SCIENTIFIC EVIDENCE FOR AND AGAINST NDES

I have done my best to keep this chapter as short as possible as I am aware that people are reading this book to understand how NDEs relate to Jesus. However, I am really into clinical and scientific research—that's my day job after all. While I have kept this chapter to a minimum, it presents a story of how the science of NDEs emerged, which may interest some readers. Nonetheless, I appreciate others may not share the same interest in these details. If you are of the latter disposition, I totally get it. Just go to the end of this chapter to the last section with the subheading "Summary of Scientific Evidence for and Against NDEs Being Real." But if you are interested in how this "paranormal" phenomenon entered mainstream research, and want to learn some interesting pieces of data, then read on.

The first scientific research studies into NDEs were of the observational type mentioned above and aimed to develop a better clinical/scientific understanding of NDEs and maybe provide information to develop a hypothesis. These were published in the early 2000s. We will now look at the highlights of the three most important of these studies that helped characterize NDEs in an objective manner, frame core clinical parameters and also provide the foundations for a hypothesis.

I will only go into the details of the first study to give a flavour—the other two studies were similar in nature but with subtle variations that provide extra detail. The design of all the studies follows a similar core format:

- Prospectively recruit patients who have survived an in-hospital CA in assigned hospitals.
- Interview the patients within certain time frames and determine if they have any recollections from their time in CA.
- Determine whether the patients who reported recollections also had an NDE using pre-determined criteria for defining an NDE.
- Identify physiological and demographic characteristics of those reporting NDEs that may differentiate them from those not having NDEs; for example, age.
- Try to characterize the underlying nature of NDEs and what they represent.

STUDY 1: NEAR DEATH EXPERIENCE IN SURVIVORS OF CARDIAC ARREST: A PROSPECTIVE STUDY IN THE NETHERLANDS[7]

The study, published in The Lancet, began in 1988 and was carried out in ten hospitals in the Netherlands. Prior to this, everything presented or published had been from retrospective studies that documented accounts from patients who already had NDEs. These are open to criticism due to factors such as patient self-selection and long periods of time between the event and the interview.

Van Lommel's study was the first prospective study to examine the phenomenon of NDEs in patients surviving cardiac arrest (CA). To be included in the study, the NDEs had to occur after study initiation and meet certain criteria.

In Van Lommel's study, CA survivors were interviewed within a few days of resuscitation. Follow-up interviews were conducted two years and eight years later. A number of baseline variables, such as demographic, pharmacological, physiological, and psychological factors experienced by CA patients were recorded and comparisons were made between patients who had NDEs and those who did not, to see if these might contribute towards people's likelihood of having an NDE. Including CA survivors who did not report an NDE is the equivalent to having a placebo in a drug trial.

NDEs were scored according to the presence and quality of ten core elements: awareness of being dead; positive emotions; out of body experience (OBE); passing along a tunnel between distinct realms; communication with light; observation of colours; meeting dead people; life review; presence of border; and sense of suddenly returning to their body.

This last list, which is very similar to the Greyson scale, may seem really odd being present in a medical scientific research study. However, this is the first study of its kind, and these are elements that had been reported from anecdotal accounts discussed previously. We will go into what these elements are and what they may mean in a lot more detail later; but for now you just need to understand that if you are going to perform a serious study on NDEs, you need to include these aspects to confirm you are looking at the same thing.

There was no attempt in this study to prove that NDEs are real, just to understand how often they are reported, the patient characteristics of those who had NDEs and whether there was any difference with those people who had not experienced an NDE. There were also some additional ideas that were explored, as we will see.

Here are highlights of, in my view, the most interesting points and a discussion of the author's comments:

- The proportion of people having a "true" NDE is in the range of 5 to 10% of patients who experience a CA and survive to be interviewed.
- Like many other researchers, he suggests that a problem with short-term memory may account for the fact that not all survivors of CA report having an NDE. This is a topic that will become very important when we consider some of the teachings of Jesus later.
- Van Lommel's hypothesis for the low incidence of NDE reports among CA survivors is partly based on the fact that likelihood of reporting an NDE in the study decreased as age increased. It is well understood that short-term memory deteriorates as we age, particularly after the age of fifty; therefore, it is certainly possible that the lower frequency of NDEs among older CA survivors may be due to having greater impairment of memory.

This study had a notable, and now famous, "veridical" (verified by a third party) OBE. In the account, a nurse removed the false teeth of a subject who was in a coma after a possible CA and being treated in the coronary care unit. She placed the teeth in a crash cart and forgot about them. A week later, when the nurse went to visit the patient in the ICU, he recognized her and told the other nurses in the room that she knew where his false teeth were. The nurse reported that he was in a coma when she had removed his teeth and could not have possibly seen or known what she did with his teeth or the other events he said he witnessed. Moreover, he was moved to another room before he came out of the coma. This is the first ever verified OBE to occur within a prospective study set up to examine NDEs. Given that this paper had to undergo peer review from professors of medicine on behalf of The Lancet, one the world's leading medical journals, this account is highly significant.

Other tidbits are as follows.

Patients with more return of spontaneous circulation (ROSC) events had a higher chance of experiencing an NDE. For instance, if they had two CAs over a period of a year, they had a higher chance of experiencing an NDE than someone who had only one CA. You may think this is obvious, but it does provide contradictory evidence to one of the hypotheses I propose later about only 10% of older people having NDEs, and it is directly relevant to Jesus' teachings that refute universalism.

The interviews done two and eight years later showed that patients who had an NDE were generally more spiritual and prone to believing in an afterlife than they had been before. In contrast, patients who had not had an NDE were more likely not to believe in the afterlife and become less interested in spirituality as time progressed.

Van Lommel notes a marked difference between the kinds of experiences described by the subjects who experienced NDEs in his study compared to those who experienced "NDE-like" experiences induced through chemical or other means in other studies researching the field. This is a common theme and something I will discuss in more detail later in this chapter. He concludes, "NDE pushes at the limits of medical ideas about the range of human consciousness and the mind–brain relationship."

My conclusions about this study?

A low percentage of patients achieving ROSC after CA have NDEs. In addition, the likelihood of experiencing—or remembering an experience—deteriorates with age. Van Lommel ascribes this to deteriorating memory in older patients. However, this is a classic case of mixing association and causation, an example being the idea that because London is in England, all people living in London must be English. In this study discussion the association is this: (1) older people have worse memory, (2) older people report NDEs fewer times than younger people, (3) therefore, the cause of the difference in NDE reports is deterioration in memory. However, the fact that older patients are less likely to recall an NDE in fact has two possible explanations:

1. Van Lommel is right. The fact that older patients have worse memory recall is the reason why older people report fewer NDEs.
2. Patients who grow older are less likely to *have* an NDE whether they remember it or not.

I find it interesting, and possibly pertinent, that during the eight years after their cardiac arrests, patients who had not experienced an NDE had become progressively less interested in spirituality. This may hint at another possible but highly controversial explanation as to why percentages of patients having NDEs after resuscitation decreases with age. While most researchers on this subject suggest that explanations are memory related—and some of the data from this study may support that—there are other pieces of data that hint at alternative explanations. This is such an important topic related specifically to what Jesus tells us about the destiny of our souls that it will have its own section later.

Another interesting finding in the study is that women are more likely to experience an NDE than men, despite the women being older. I have often noticed that many churches have a higher proportion of women than men, and this is borne out in data from Pew Research Center's 2014 Religious Landscape Study: "American women are more likely than American men to say they pray daily (64% vs. 47%) and attend religious services at least once a week (40% vs. 32%)."

I have often pondered why this might be. Might there be genetic reasons for women showing a greater predisposition toward spirituality? Historically, men have been more likely than women to be involved directly in hand-to-hand violent struggle. It could be argued that the most successful would be those who are best at winning, and that to win you may be less likely to show empathy or compassion for your opponent's suffering. If this psychological disposition for showing compassion is genetic, it would be more likely to be passed on to the next generation.

The next generation of course has an equal chance of being male or female, so should this lack of compassion not be passed on to both sexes? Maybe, but it is known that certain traits and mutations are present only on the Y chromosome, and therefore passed only from father to son. This is all speculation but, in my experience, spiritual people seem more compassionate, and the finding from Van Lommel's study that women are more likely to have an NDE than men may be evidence that men are less able to remember or experience spiritual occurrences. We will venture into the poorly charted area of spirituality and genetics later.

STUDY 2: THE INCIDENCE AND CORRELATES OF NEAR DEATH EXPERIENCES IN A CARDIAC CARE UNIT[8]

Dr. Greyson is one of the most widely published researchers on NDEs in the established literature. He has a host of citations to his name. He is also the creator of the Greyson NDE scale, an interview tool used by researchers to establish whether the experience is an NDE or otherwise. The interviewer asks twelve questions related to specific elements of NDEs. For example, one question is, "Did you have a feeling of peace or pleasantness?" The answer is then graded with a score from zero for neither, one for relief or calmness, and two for incredible peace or pleasantness. The scores are added up after all twelve questions are asked, and if the subject scores greater than seven, the experience is classified as an NDE.

This study, like the others, had a similar design as the Van Lommel study, except that a number of cardiac "events" were included, not just CA. Here are the highlights of a few interesting findings and my comments on some of the conclusions:

- NDEs were most common in those who had survived a cardiac arrest (10%), compared to 2% of the entire cardiac "event" cohort, many of whom were not close to death. This is the first study to show that NDEs are associated with the patient actually being close to death or being temporarily clinically dead.
- Patients either reported a robust NDE as per the Greyson scale, nothing at all, or something that was not remotely close to an NDE despite all other circumstances being similar. There was not a spectrum of scores, something you might expect if this was a physiological or pharmacological effect.
- NDErs reported more prior paranormal experiences than non-NDErs. There are three possible explanations:

    - Persons who believe they had a prior paranormal experience are more likely to report NDEs.
    - Persons who have NDEs are more likely to interpret past experiences as paranormal.
    - Subjects who have NDEs report more prior paranormal experiences because they are more "spiritual." There may be something intrinsic about them that enables them to have these types of experiences.

STUDY 3: A QUALITATIVE AND QUANTITATIVE STUDY OF THE INCIDENCE, FEATURES AND ETIOLOGY OF NEAR DEATH EXPERIENCES IN CARDIAC ARREST SURVIVORS[9]

The author of this study is none other than Dr. Sam Parnia, whom I mentioned in this book's introduction.

It was conducted at Southampton General Hospital in the UK over the course of one year at the end of the 1990s. In addition to the similarities of design of the studies, this study was one of a handful to prospectively deploy the use of "targets"—images on cards placed on high shelves in the resuscitation suite—to prove whether OBEs are indeed quantifiably genuine. According to Dr. Parnia:

> If OBEs are indeed veridical, anybody who claimed to have left their body and be near the ceiling during a resuscitation attempt would be expected to identify those targets. If, however, such perceptions are psychological, then one would not expect the targets to be identified.

This statement is obviously the beginning of a hypothesis and experiment to validate it, but is problematic for various reasons. One of these is that it is a rather crude summary of the experiment and not a fully developed hypothesis with respect to validation of the OBE. But it was a starting point in terms of experiments and, given this was in the 1990s, I do not think anyone at the time could have done better, and Dr. Parnia is to be highly commended for undertaking a study of this kind in the first place. As it turns out, Parnia's comments about subjects observing targets was a moot point.

To briefly summarize, only four out of sixty-three CA subjects (6.3%) had an NDE according to the Greyson scale. No significant differences in psychological or physiological factors were observed between those who experienced an NDE and those who did not. Given that four subjects reported an NDE, one might hope at least one subject would report an OBE, as about 25% of NDErs report OBEs. However, not only did no subjects report seeing the target cards, but no OBEs of any kind were reported. This is why Parnia's statement is moot with respect to this study.

MOVING BEYOND OBSERVATION

By 2008 an impasse had been reached in the evolution of NDE science. The three early prospective studies—and a multitude of other studies published in non-mainstream journals and books—were all saying the same things:

1. NDEs occur in about 5–10% of patients who survive a cardiac arrest.
2. NDErs report a number of core elements with a subset reporting visual and auditory OBEs.
3. A significant number of OBEs are veridical. Namely, the observations made during the OBE were verified by another person, or persons, who were often credible healthcare professionals with no personal relationship to the subject. One of these was reported within the setting of a clinical trial, and while this was not strictly speaking "scientifically verified" (proven using the scientific method), it does carry more weight than anecdotal accounts outside of a research setting.

In a normal world, despite the lack of scientifically measured proof, this should have been enough evidence to convince most reasonable people that NDEs and OBEs are real. Plus, in turn, all the implications that follow from that, including proving that humans have a consciousness that can survive death and "escape" the confines of the body. But, as I have noted, we live in a world ruled, for the most part, by materialist philosophy and its adherents.

Numerous arguments have been presented by atheists within the academic establishment to explain away these results. I will summarize the key ones shortly, however, not one of these arguments properly addresses the impossibility of someone seeing or hearing things outside of their body while they are unconscious.

The impasse we have existed in since the late 2000s is that the skeptical academic establishment want absolute proof that NDEs and OBEs are real and do not view human testimony from reliable sources as sufficient. Since then, those who are interested in this subject have been waiting for studies to provide scientific proof one way or the other. They want evidence generated using the scientific method of observation > hypothesis generation > experimentation. How would that look in relation to this scientific controversy?

- **Observation**: On dying (cessation of heart and brain activity) some people are able to observe themselves and their surroundings from outside of their bodies despite their brains being incapable of sustaining conscious activity.
- **Dualist Hypothesis explaining observation**: The consciousness is a separate entity from the body, independent of brain function, and is able to survive death for an indeterminate period. (The competing materialistic hypothesis is that the brain generates the experience – but this is disproven by default if observations are made from outside of the body).
- **Experiment**: To test this hypothesis, you would need to devise an experiment that created and monitored the same conditions of clinical death, and a scientifically robust way of validating any recollections from patients who report an OBE.

The most obvious setting in which to conduct this experiment is in the resuscitation suites of large hospitals that frequently have patients who go into CA. Determining the status of the heart using ECG is routine in this instance, so establishing the time during which a patient had no heartbeat is straightforward. As for EEG monitoring, this is not routine early in the process of trying to resuscitate a patient. Once a patient has achieved ROSC and is in an induced coma, then EEG will be added to the measurements, but it is not routine while CPR is being performed on a patient who is clinically dead.

This has always been a point that skeptics have pounced on. How do we know the brain is not active during CPR? Surely this could be the cause of NDEs? Surely OBEs are just the brain picking up sights and sounds and then turning them into some sort of OBE-like memory?

This is where the second element of the experiment—the verification of OBE reports from patients—must be designed with particular care. You have to create a way of validating what the patient claimed to see, while clinically dead, that will survive the scrutiny of the most pedantic skeptic.

Here we go back to Sam Parnia's study that we just covered. This was one of the first attempts to try to prove OBEs. Cards were placed high up on shelves that would be visible only to someone looking down from the ceiling—as is often the case for those who report OBEs while clinically dead. It was a very crude way of doing the experiment, but at the time was probably the best available. The idea was that if a patient had a memory of seeing a card bearing an image, then the OBE was (scientifically) proven.

At this point, given that we had gathered a sufficient amount of observations from research studies, and have a potential hypothesis explaining these observations, one would have expected that research would have switched entirely to the experiment phase of gathering evidence to support the hypothesis. Within the NDE community, it was hoped that the next big study announced to investigate NDEs would indeed focus on this.

THE AWARE STUDY[10]

Dr. Parnia did not launch the AWARE study until 2008, seven years after publishing the data from his initial study, possibly because he faced significant headwinds. Some in the medical scientific community opposed his work on NDEs, regarding it as frivolous or even quackery. He did not have big funding from the pharmaceutical industry, but did receive support from the resuscitation council and from organizations such as the John Templeton and Nour foundations. More importantly he had to gain the support of numerous co-investigators from other hospitals to ensure there would be sufficiently speedy recruitment.

The primary aim of the study was to establish the incidence of awareness and range of mental experiences during resuscitation and to establish a way of verifying reports of visual and auditory awareness during CA. Note the use of the word "establish." This study was designed to look at how to prove whether or not OBEs are real; it does not set out with the explicit aim of actually proving.

The study was a multicenter, international, prospective observational study. It took place in twenty hospitals around the world, but mostly in the UK and US and adopted a similar design to previous studies.

To validate the visual component of NDEs, each hospital installed 50–100 shelves in locations where CPR was likely to occur, such as resuscitation suites and ICUs. Each shelf had different images including such things as animals, religious symbols, people, and newspaper headlines that were visible only from above if viewed from the ceiling.

The initial goal was to recruit 1,000 to 1,500 patients. This is the powering aspect of the study and on the face of it this seemed to be a sufficient number of survivors to generate enough recollections of awareness that would better characterize the experiences.

Why is that the case?

Data from previous studies showed about 5–10% of CA survivors have an NDE, and of these, about 20–25% have a visual OBE. Based on that, if one thousand CA survivors were recruited and interviewed, you would predict about 50–100 NDEs and 10–25 OBEs. If that many people reported OBEs, and if OBEs were indeed real, at least a few of those would catch sight of and recall a target image on a shelf.

That is not what happened, though.

Dr. Parnia presented the AWARE I study results on a poster at a cardiology conference in 2014 and, shortly after, published them in the medical journal Resuscitation.

The study "recruited" 2,060 patients, which was considerably more than the initial 1000–1,500 patients originally planned. If the dualist hypothesis outlined above is valid, you would have expected at least half a dozen patients would have verified OBEs by observing and identifying the images on the cards.

The result? There was only one verified OBE, and it was not verified using the cards.

So, what went wrong?

After an in-depth review, it became obvious that AWARE I had been extremely unlikely to verify OBEs. First, were there really enough subjects "recruited" into the study to sufficiently power it?

The answer is no and is related to the reason I put "recruited" in quotes.

The vast majority of the 2,060 patients did not survive long enough to be interviewed by the study investigators. Only 140 patients reached the first of the interview stages.

That's right, only 140 CA survivors were actually interviewed.

If the study had been designed around "validating" (or otherwise) the specific hypothesis I propose, then the minimum requirements for being included in the analysis would be that they survived long enough to complete the interviews—something I had assumed was the case before the results were presented. With only 140 subjects, this study was insufficiently powered, which made it only marginally more informative than the studies that had occurred previously. The number of NDEs and OBEs was very much in line with what had been observed before. But the question remains "Why wasn't either of the OBEs verified by the patients seeing the cards?"

First, using target cards is a relatively limited and crude way of verifying OBEs, as not all patients who have an OBE report seeing themselves from directly above. Sometimes they are standing beside themselves or are in the corner of the room. It is hard to estimate what the chances are of someone experiencing an OBE and having it from the right vantage point to see the cards.

Second, due to the fact that OBEs are an unusual and unexpected event, it is possible, maybe even likely, that the experiencer may not have the "presence of mind" to notice the cards, even if they are in a position where they are able to see them. Given that only two people reported OBEs, it is unlikely that one or both of the two patients who had an OBE would have seen and remembered the cards—if they had even been in rooms with cards in the first place.

Third, and of most relevance to answering the question of why no patients identified the cards, is the fact that despite there being over one thousand "card shelves" in multiple hospital sites in acute and emergency wards, 78% of the CAs that occurred during this study occurred in patients' rooms without the shelves. As a result, neither of the patients who reported OBEs was in a room with cards present!

The only verified OBE in the AWARE I study was that of a man who made observations from the corner of a room while his body was unconscious on a bed. In his interview he was able to identify staff who were present in the room only while he was unconscious, as well as being able to describe in detail many of the procedures that were performed. His accounts were verified by members of the team who performed the emergency resuscitation process. This is a very good example of a well-documented, humanly verified, veridical OBE, but with the exception that it was recorded in the setting of a prospective clinical study looking out for this effect, and that the events he reported were correlated with the time that he was reported to be clinically dead.

Given the context of the setting of the recorded OBE, there are arguments for and against naming this a "scientifically" validated OBE.

What is the argument for it? The study was created using the scientific method, conducted in a scientific manner in a research setting. An OBE was confirmed by reliable professional human observers and for the first time the observations made by the subject were matched with the time he would not have been able to make or record observations, since he was clinically dead.

The argument against it is that it failed to verify OBEs using the pre-specified technique designed for the purpose of validating visual observations during CPR.

As a scientist, I am of the view that the latter position is correct. While one of the OBEs was verified in an extremely credible manner, it was not, from the strict definition, "scientifically" verified. It is important to note that the OBE was not scientifically disproved either—the study just failed to collect enough information to allow a conclusion to be drawn on this subject.

To produce scientific verification of whether or not OBEs are genuine experiences in which the consciousness observes events from outside of the body would require setting up a study with the explicit aim of validating the observations of patients and providing evidence to support the hypothesis I lay out above, and then powering the study to ensure sufficient patients were interviewed after ROSC. In reality, Dr. Parnia did not have the resources or the time to conduct a study that would have needed to be at least ten times larger than it was. The largest hurdle facing Dr. Parnia was in fact the lack of people surviving CAs.

Having learned about his techniques from AWARE I, Sam Parnia went on to perform the follow-up study, AWARE II. Did he learn the lesson about powering, though?

AWARE II[11]

The primary goal of the study was to collect different measures of what happens to the brain during resuscitation and thereby assess the health and activity of the brain during and after CPR. This is largely dependent on how much oxygenated blood is reaching the brain. The secondary goal of the study was to ascertain the presence of consciousness during CA and the occurrence of OBEs and NDEs.

The study sought to recruit 1,000–1,500 patients and had slightly tightened the inclusion criteria—the specific characteristics of the subjects that could be enrolled. Subjects needed to have an in-hospital CA when the AWARE research team were present and the AWARE study equipment was in place during CPR and before ROSC. The team also made several important alterations to the methodology used to verify any potential OBE reports. They abandoned the shelves with cards for a much more modern and scientifically robust technique.

Special crash carts or trolleys that carry equipment commonly used for emergency resuscitation were designed for AWARE II to monitor patients during CPR. These carts carried equipment investigators would use to analyze activity in the patient's brain post-CA and during resuscitation. Then they would correlate the information with any reports of conscious activity and, alongside ascertaining clinical implications, potentially verify, or discount, any reported OBEs.

These crash carts included oximetry machines, which measure oxygen levels and thereby blood flow to the brain, and EEG monitors, which show brain activity. They are the key physiological parameters that determine the brain's ability to generate, or host, consciousness. There was also equipment to produce visual and auditory stimuli during resuscitation to assess the patient's external awareness during any conscious episodes. This included headphones to place on the patient's ears to convey loud sounds and an iPad fixed to a pole above head height with the screen facing the ceiling, which would produce random images only visible from above the iPad's screen.

Importantly, when it comes to inclusion criteria, the patients would be included in the study only if the crash cart had arrived before the patient was resuscitated. This was an attempt to avoid the situation that happened in AWARE I, where OBEs occurred without the images being present.

Of greater importance is the fact that because this study is primarily designed for assessing the health of the brain during and after CPR, it does not exclude patients who die before an interview can be conducted.

Once again, it appears there is no specific hypothesis relating to OBEs in this iteration of AWARE.

The results of Aware II are as follows:

Of 567 subjects "recruited," *only 28/53 completed interviews*, of which 6/28 (21%) had a transcendent experience (NDE). Importantly (and unsurprisingly), no one had explicit recall of the projected images or auditory cues.

Once again, this study suffered from the same fundamental issue as previous studies; namely, low numbers of interviews due to the low survival rates of people experiencing CA. The truth is that this is a worse outcome than AWARE I, but it does not in any way imply that OBEs or NDEs are not real.

One aspect of the results that was intriguing was the EEG substudy, and the conclusions that Sam Parnia drew from this data.

According to the authors, EEG data "consistent with consciousness" was recorded in patients up to 60 minutes after CA began. However, it is important to note that the ability to interpret EEG data, which consists of output of electrical signals of varying frequencies from electrodes placed on the scalp, is not yet an exact science. Different frequencies of signal are associated with different types of neuronal activity, but are rarely unique to one type. For instance, higher-level conscious activity is often associated with gamma frequencies (higher frequencies of greater than 40 Hz) but these frequencies are also associated with muscle contractions.

Despite the fact this discovery was groundbreaking, the most important aspect of the EEG findings boils down to whether or not any of the patients who reported NDEs also had EEG output consistent with consciousness. If there was a single patient who had EEG data consistent with consciousness while having an NDE, then at the very least it would be possible for skeptics to claim there is an association between these experiences and brain activity. If this were the case, there are two possible explanations:

1. The materialist explanation: the brain is causing the NDE; thus, supporting the hypothesis that the soul is not an independent entity.
2. The non-materialist explanation: as the consciousness is leaving the brain, it causes an increase in brain activity. Parnia refers to this as disinhibition (I call it "the soul packing its bags and leaving" hypothesis!).

However, neither of these is relevant in this instance since the paper states, "Two of the 28 interviewed subjects had EEG data but weren't among those with explicit cognitive recall."

This is the money line, the one that shoots down any materialist attempts to use this study to say that NDEs are proven to be a result of brain activity: *none of the 11 subjects who reported conscious recollections had EEG data that showed markers of consciousness.*

I like the idea of the disinhibition hypothesis proposed by Dr. Parnia to explain EEG signals during CPR, because at some point the consciousness must separate from the brain, possibly causing EEG activity. However, I am of the view that the EEG activity observed in this study is more likely related to the possibility that during CPR there may be times that sufficient oxygenated blood reaches the brain causing it to start "rebooting."

Ultimately, the results from the first two AWARE studies are disappointing, due entirely to the fact that they were not really experiments set up to prove the OBE hypothesis, but just advanced observational studies and pilot studies assessing methods for just such an experiment. However, there is still hope that we may not have to wait so long for a scientifically verified OBE.

AWARE III

This is a study in patients who undergo hypothermic surgery, also conducted by the AWARE group, which is perhaps one of the more promising studies in terms of getting verified OBEs. In this kind of surgery, critical work is done on the heart or brain where the surgeon must cool the body temperature down to the point that the patient experiences deep hypothermic circulatory arrest. This causes the patient's heart to stop beating and the brain to stop functioning. This state can be maintained for about an hour without any ill effects because the cells in the brain are cooled sufficiently to avoid any damage. Once the hour is up, the patient is slowly warmed up and revived. It is a well-established, relatively safe, and reliable technique.

Interestingly, and perhaps unsurprisingly given that the patients are, in essence, clinically dead, there have been a number of reports of OBEs during these medical procedures. Pam Reynolds's NDE, mentioned earlier, and in the next section, is one example. Another was noted in a study in Montreal specifically set up to investigate this phenomenon.[12] This study also found that about 10% of people had conscious recollections that mirrored results from "natural" cardiac arrest NDEs.

As AWARE III gets under way, Dr. Parnia is going to use his setup with the iPad and headphones in hypothermic surgeries. As the patients will almost certainly survive and might have consented to the study prior to "dying," they may even be asked to look for the iPad, if they have an OBE.

2022 CONSENSUS STATEMENT[2]

Before we look at the scientific evidence against NDEs, it is important to address another publication that Parnia and other eminent NDE researchers published in early 2022. This was a consensus statement that attempted to summarize the state of the field and to clearly define the characteristics of what differentiates "authentic" NDEs and OBEs from other experiences. With all the observational data from the many studies now conducted, this paper included a lot more detail about the nature of NDEs, the clinical circumstances, the potential explanations and suggestions on how to proceed with future research. The paper concludes with the following statement:

> Finally, we suggest that although systematic studies have not been able to absolutely prove the reality or meaning of patients' experiences and claims of awareness in relation to death, it has been impossible to disclaim them either. Clearly, the recalled experience surrounding death now merits further genuine empirical investigation without prejudice.

In other words, watch this space.

There are two aspects of the consensus paper that I sharply disagree with, and the first of those, the idea that an experience can be an "authentic NDE" only if it is positive, goes against the paper Parnia cites to generate this definition. It is possibly one of the most egregious examples of confirmation bias (I am struggling to use polite terms) that I have seen. I will go into details of this when we discuss NDEs to do with hell.

The second aspect relates to memory. Both of these issues will be covered in sections later but, suffice to say, it appears that Parnia wants to believe only in a universe where everyone gets a happy ending and will include only evidence that confirms this belief—or even possibly distort evidence against it. This is of significant concern given the public profile of Dr. Parnia. Therefore, I feel it is important to address his position in the consensus paper.

The saying "The road to hell is paved with good intentions" could not be more appropriate since, by narrowing the future of research in this field to only positive experiences when there are quite clearly also hell-like experiences that share many of the other key characteristics of NDEs, he is creating a very dangerous precedent. This potentially denies humankind extremely important information about the future of the soul. As I have said before, I have a lot of respect for Parnia and the team who work with him, but on this issue and on the issue of memory, I strongly disagree. That is why this book is so important—few other writers with a scientific background, or from the NDE field, are discussing what is empirical evidence of a potentially catastrophic outcome for a significant percentage of people. Jesus very clearly predicts hell for human beings who do not follow his instructions.

I will return to this later, but now for a discussion of the scientific evidence against NDEs.

IS THERE SCIENTIFIC EVIDENCE AGAINST NDES BEING REAL?

Skeptics cite a number of scientific studies or observations to discredit the idea that OBEs and NDEs are real. These can be divided into two categories:

1. The patients' experiences were the result of some internal process arising from the brain's last firings after the heart stopped or due to CPR. This hypothesis – that the brain produces the experience - arises from three pieces of related evidence from different studies:
    - EEG signals of a frequency potentially associated with consciousness (gamma frequency) have been observed in rats for up to 30 seconds after inducing CA.[13]
    - In another study conducted by the same University of Michigan research group[14] led by Limo Borjigin, a small number of coma patients showed strong EEG activity for a minute or two after withdrawal of life support (oxygen), but prior to CA. This researcher has been misleading in her claims about her research. She has said that EEG activity associated with consciousness occurred during CA. This claim has been slavishly repeated by articles in the media, including on CNN, the BBC, the Guardian and even scientific American. However, they are misleading. All meaningful EEG signals ceased entirely before any of the patients' hearts stopped beating. She either does not understand the meaning of the term "cardiac arrest" or is being economical with the truth. Moreover, while there were brief bursts of gamma activity prior to CA that might conceivably have been indicative of consciousness, in none of these cases was an NDE or OBE reported that

could be correlated with this EEG activity. Therefore, any (false) conclusions drawn or assertions made are based on speculation.

- The data from the AWARE II publication suggests that in a small number of patients, CPR can produce sufficient EEG activity to allow the theoretical possibility of consciousness occurring, but this has not so far been correlated with any recollections of consciousness. Any suggestion that consciousness did or even could occur under these circumstances is pure speculation, let alone the idea that these rare gamma signals are evidence of NDEs.

It is absolutely fundamental to understand that there is no evidence from any study published to date (October 2024), whether it be in animals or humans, that brain activity around the time of death and reports of NDEs are associated. To date there has not been a single report of an NDE with accompanying EEG activity. You might have heard of the expression "Association is not causation." Well, here there is not even any association, let alone a jot of evidence of causation. To this latter point, even if someone who had reported an NDE had EEG activity associated with it, the cause of this association is still a matter of speculation. It could be the "consciousness packing its bags and leaving"—the disinhibition/disassociation hypothesis mentioned before. Or it could be that the recollection of an NDE is indeed caused by brain activity, as suggested by materialists.

2. The second path of reasoning that skeptics follow to try to discredit the "supernatural" explanation for NDEs is that NDE-like experiences can be induced naturally using drugs or other techniques. They claim that NDEs around death are therefore just the result of some

pharmacological or physiological effects on the brain:
- Drugs used in the ER are causing NDEs. However, experiments using the kinds of drugs used in an ER if a patient is having a CA, when used in healthy volunteers who are not having a CA, show they are not associated with NDE-like reports.
- It is true that NDE-like experiences, as well as OBEs, have been associated with the use of some psychedelic drugs; electrical stimulations of the brain; syncope (fainting); epileptic fits; or certain religious meditation techniques. Since none of these patients were dead, it could be argued that OBEs are not unique to NDEs.

Do either of these explanations—or any others—discredit the idea that NDEs or OBEs are real and provide evidence that the consciousness survives death?

No. Clearly in the first case, the drugs used in the ER have been scientifically proven not to be causing NDEs. With regard to the second type of scenario the research that suggested that any of the patients had OBEs described very different types of experience to those reported by NDErs. Any reports of genuine OBEs in these circumstances were not documented let alone scientifically validated, or indeed veridical (validated by a third-party observer) and are usually just distortions of visual perspective, rather than viewing one's body completely from the outside. Moreover, even if they were validated OBEs, this would in fact prove that the consciousness is able to momentarily separate itself from the body as a result of pharmacological, electrical, or neurological interference. If anything, such reports would reinforce the argument that the consciousness is a separate entity to the body and that the body is only a "host."

Some skeptics argue that the AWARE studies themselves are evidence that

OBEs and NDEs are not real because they failed to produce a scientifically verified result. I hope by now it is obvious from the preceding sections that it is very clear why neither of the AWARE studies was likely to produce many, if any, scientifically validated visual OBEs. Quite simply the inclusion criteria for the studies were not focused on recruiting sufficient patients to reach the necessary interview stages to make it even remotely likely that a visual OBE would be verified. Such a study would need to follow tens of thousands of CA patients because so many of them fail to survive. There are only so many crash carts with iPads, oximetry equipment and personnel trained to use them that a team like Dr. Parnia's can have. If more hospitals took part, and the inclusion criteria were changed, then AWARE II may well produce scientifically verified visual OBEs, as well as auditory OBEs. It is interesting that some groups, led by materialist skeptics (or physicalists as some prefer to be called), such as Charlotte Marshall in Liege University, Belgium, are reported to be creating studies using a similar set up as Parnia's to disprove the dualist explanation of NDEs and OBEs. They could use either (1) a hypothesis like the dualist one I propose and disprove it, or (2) create a competing hypothesis, which they validate, maybe something along the lines of NDEs being purely a function of the last firings of a dying brain, and any reports of OBEs are memories created during these firings. If the second hypothesis is true, then people who report NDEs will not have scientifically validated OBEs.

I suspect they will go the former route, as disproving a hypothesis is allowed. To do that you deliberately underpower the study so that there are insufficient people having interviews to report a validated OBE. As they are using only one ER room with hidden images, they may indeed be designing this to "disprove" any hypothesis based on Platonic dualism (the soul lives in the body and the two are separate but united in this life). However, would it not be delicious irony if this researcher's study produced the first scientifically validated OBE? It would certainly be regarded as extremely strong evidence given the fact it was set up by a skeptic. I am not holding my breath, though.

In summary, a lack of a scientifically verified positive result is not evidence of a negative result, and in the absence of strong evidence to show that OBEs are indeed the product of a misfiring brain or drugs, the only conclusion to be drawn about evidence against OBEs (and NDEs) being real is that there is none. None.

Related to this is the well-established fact that no one has ever provided a validated theory or scientific explanation of how the brain might generate consciousness. It is often referred to as one of the last remaining mysteries of science. It is merely a materialist assumption that the brain produces consciousness, based on materialistic beliefs; namely, that there is no such thing as the "soul" or "God" and that every observation has a physical or natural explanation. This is absolutely an assumption and not based on evidence. It is in fact just as scientific to postulate that consciousness is a separate entity to the brain as it is to postulate it is produced by the brain, but only if you ignore the evidence presented previously. Indeed, if you remove your own bias, when you consider the fact that there is no evidence or viable working theory that accounts for how the brain would produce consciousness, it is perfectly rational to hold the belief that the brain simply hosts consciousness.

SUMMARY OF SCIENTIFIC EVIDENCE FOR AND AGAINST NDES BEING REAL

Professional clinical and scientific researchers have made great progress in characterising NDEs, and creating methods to validate OBEs. However, there is still not a single scientifically validated OBE because most patients who have a CA do not survive, despite advances in modern medicine. As a result of this poor survival rate, insufficient numbers of patients have been interviewed after ROSC in any of these studies to "validate" or disprove the hypothesis using the scientific method.

While these studies, set in professional research settings, and published in major reputable scientific journals, have produced two veridical OBEs (verified by attending HCPs in the context of a research study), they were not OBEs proven using the scientific method. Specifically, they were not proven using an experiment in which predefined analytical methods were designed to capture and validate these reports. Due to the small number of survivors, there have so far been no reports of a visual OBE in a setting where the equipment to validate such a report was even present. In AWARE I, both OBEs occurred in a room with no image shelf; and in AWARE II, there were no OBEs reported at all due to the tiny number of survivors interviewed.

Regarding evidence against NDEs being real, this mostly comprises the extrapolating of results of residual brain activity in rats up to 30 seconds after CA as being evidence of consciousness and therefore the capability for the brain to generate an NDE. There is no equivalent data in humans during CA, except for occasional bursts of activity during CPR where blood flow possibly reaches sufficient levels to "reboot" the brain. Neither of these types of activity has ever been associated with a report of an NDE. Other evidence cited is that NDE-like experiences can be induced using various methods such as psychedelics. While there may be some truth in this, none of these has produced a veridical OBE, and if they did, such a result would in fact be supportive of the dualist (soul vs. body) understanding and that the consciousness is a separate entity to the brain. In conclusion, while NDEs have not been proven "real" by the scientific method, there is no evidence at all showing that NDEs or OBEs are not "real"; that is, that the consciousness doesn't leave the body at (clinical) death.

So, if NDEs have not been proven real using the scientific method, why do I state in the introduction that NDEs have been proven real beyond any reasonable doubt?

Because they have! Reasonable doubt is when sufficient empirical evidence has been provided so that no other conclusion is plausible. We have a mountain of reliable empirical evidence. Read on.

CHAPTER 4: PROOF BEYOND REASONABLE DOUBT

DO WE REALLY NEED A "SCIENTIFICALLY" VERIFIED OBE?

This is a question I have touched on before and will refer back to again at times. As a physical scientist who works in medicine, until recently I have been 100% confident of the results of an experiment only when it is confirmed by technological measurements. For instance, during my years working in HIV, we would use measurements of viral load (amount of virus in a milliliter of blood), and CD4 count (numbers of the CD4 immune cells in a millilter of blood) to measure the effectiveness of a drug.

When I worked in Alzheimer's, there were two ways of testing the effectiveness of a drug. One was using MRI and PET scans to see the change in brain structure and presence of two types of protein, Amyloid and Tau. The other was a cognitive test usually carried out by a psychiatrist. Both of these are highly objective, quantitative and scientific—even the cognitive test, which uses a battery of questions that track changes in the patient's ability to remember things and to process information. The answers to these questions are objectively measurable. For example, in the Mini Mental State Exam (MMSE) you are asked to remember three words at the end of the meeting that were read out loud at the start. There is no subjective interpretation from the psychiatrist: the score for this segment of the test is 0–3.

The results from any of these tests I have described are not questioned, as they have been validated in studies and, especially with scans and blood tests, avoid any human potential interference through subjective interpretation or manipulation. Of course, statisticians can fiddle with numbers and create different impressions, but such antics are easily exposed by the eagle eyed.

All of the therapy areas I have worked in up to this point in my career have had scientific objective measures to validate results. However, more recently I was in discussions with an organization that has developed a drug that treats depression. In this instance, as with Alzheimer's, a psychiatrist will have a battery of questions to ask a patient. But, unlike the cognitive tests used in Alzheimer's, which have clear, objectively measurable responses to each question, the answers are much more down to subjective interpretation by the patient or psychiatrist. For instance, when using the Montgomery–Åsberg Depression Rating Scale (MADRS), a patient may be asked to describe their state of inner tension, which can cover any number of symptoms, including feelings of ill-defined discomfort, edginess, inner turmoil, mental tension mounting to panic, dread, and so on.

These qualitative measures are completely unlike any tests I have relied on before to "validate" or disprove a hypothesis about a drug. They are subjective descriptors that rely entirely on human testimony and observation, and yet leading doctors, scientists, health bodies, insurance companies, government regulators, and so on, will accept the results from these questionnaires as having objective definitive meaning regarding the effectiveness of drugs that target depression. In other words, the medical, scientific, and academic establishment accept these results as being reliable *empirical* evidence despite their being entirely based on subjective human testimony. (The same applies outside medicine – in law, history, journalism etc).

Maybe you can see where I am going with this!

There are countless OBEs that have been recalled by patients after suffering CA, and have been corroborated by healthcare professionals, many of whom were licensed physicians. How is this so different from the results of a clinical trial in depression, or indeed a psychiatrist conducting an MADRS test on a patient for the purpose of an insurance claim for medication or a period of absence? You have the following two criteria that define an HCP veridfied OBE:

- A subject accurately describing things they saw while "out of their bodies" that they could not possibly have seen with their physical bodies. They rarely go straight to the local TV station and recount their story, or even write about it. They will usually tell hospital staff first.
- These recollections are then verified as accurate, and only possible if the patient had indeed been out of their body, by reliable rational scientifically minded professionals involved in the case. These professionals have nothing to gain by confirming these recollections, and indeed may be the subject of derision from colleagues.

Just as with measuring depression, you have a subjective patient account and an HCP evaluating that account. We have thousands of these.

Below are seven well-known cases that are condensed from the full accounts to capture the key criteria that cause them to be fully validated

OBEs. Their two criteria are (1) an observation by a patient of a specific object, procedure, or event they claimed to see while they were having their OBE and that happened during CA or in a coma following CA, and (2) the account was confirmed by an identifiable HCP and, ideally, the HCP stated that this was possible only if the patient had indeed had an OBE as their eyes were closed and their vitals pointed to an absence of physical consciousness.

While these seven cases are well known, there are countless others. Over one hundred are presented in the book *The Self Does Not Die* by Titus Rivas. I have used this book as my main reference source due to the fact that all the cases are well documented and were investigated by the authors, who interviewed all the witnesses where possible, including HCPs, involved in the confirmed OBEs. However, I have been familiar with many of these cases over the years and most are presented elsewhere. These hundred-odd are just the tip of the iceberg—they just happened to have HCPs who were prepared to go on the record and had sufficiently robust corroborating evidence. I recommend buying the book as a reference source if you are interested in this area. A couple of these cases have been mentioned before.

PAM REYNOLDS (SINGER/SONGWRITER 1956-2010)

Circumstances: Occurred in 1991 at the Barrow Neurological Institute during brain surgery while Reynolds was in a state of hypothermic cardiac arrest. Both her ECG and EEG were flatlining. The operating physician was neurosurgeon Dr. Robert Spetzler.

The two criteria qualifying it as an HCP verified OBE (as defined above) were as follows: (1) Reynolds had an OBE in which she saw a part of the operation on her brain, and specifically saw highly specialized equipment (a saw that looked like a toothbrush) being used, as well as other details that would have required observing the procedure from outside of her body. Moreover, she heard detailed discussions about the procedure that would have been impossible to hear naturally due to headphones being in her ears that played loud sounds and were designed to completely exclude external noise. (2) The account was confirmed by Robert Spetzler, a pioneer of the hypothermic CA method, and an internationally respected neurosurgeon. He discounted the possibility that she might have guessed these things from watching TV shows or reading up on the surgical techniques. He could not provide a "normal explanation" for what had occurred.

DR. LLOYD RUDY'S CASE

I first came across this on YouTube. Its authenticity struck me because it was buried in a channel for people interested in dental surgery and was a spontaneous account of an OBE given to the channel's host in 2011 by the highly respected, well-known cardiac surgeon Dr. Lloyd Rudy. During the interview, they also discussed cardiac problems related to dental infections. All the other videos, which averaged about 300 views, were of the same format with the same host. This was not a channel devoted to NDEs, of which there are many. Despite its esoteric location, the video had had millions of views by the time I first came across it. In this instance, we do not know the identity of the patient, and it was Lloyd Rudy who reported the account, not long before his own death in 2012.

Circumstances: Occurred on a Christmas Day in an unspecified year in a hospital in Great Falls, USA. An oral infection had spread to a heart valve of the patient, resulting in Dr. Rudy's performing cardiac surgery. The surgery seemed to fail and the life-support machines were turned off. The various staff had begun leaving the theater. Suddenly, after the patient's chest had been sown up ready for autopsy, some of the patient's vitals started to return. Once all the staff had rushed back to the theater, the patient's blood pressure and heart rate were normalized. He had effectively come back from the dead with no CPR. It is very rare, but does happen, and may account for some of the rare historic NDEs prior to the invention of CPR. The patient had been completely unconscious during the surgery and was in a coma for two days after the restoration of vital functions.

The two criteria were as follows: (1) The patient reported a number of incidents during the surgery that he could not have seen, including seeing a series of post-it notes on a monitor. These notes were put on the monitor for Dr. Rudy by a nurse who had taken messages he needed to respond to after the surgery. They were placed there after the surgery began and removed straight after it was finished. (2) Given this account was actually provided by Dr. Rudy, this criterion is already fulfilled. He stated there was no way the patient could naturally have seen this as the patient "was out" before the operation began.

This discussion between Dr. Rudy and the interviewer, who is a dental surgeon, is very much an aside to the original purpose of their discussion, and the way they talk about it is as though it were a very strange event that has no explanation. Two highly respected medical professionals going on the record in a completely authentic way.

DR. CHRIS YERINGTON'S CASE

This is another case of a physician providing a report of an OBE almost as an aside. It was in response to a question put to him: "As an anaesthesiologist, what has been your strangest experience while trying to put someone under?" This is possibly the most astonishing verified OBE of all.

Circumstances: A patient referred to as Frank arrived at Ohio State University Hospital sometime in late 2003 or early 2004, with vital signs so bad he was effectively dead on arrival. After placing Frank into hypothermic CA for a long period, he was wheeled into ICU, where he was expected to die. Dr. Yerington returned to the hospital a day or so later to find that Frank had staged a full recovery.

The two criteria were as follows: (1) Frank recognised Dr. Yerington and told him about his OBE, where he had witnessed the attempts to save his life, and noted something especially striking—he had been stuck on the ceiling for a long time and had read and memorized the serial numbers on three lights in the operating room. He also recalled conversations that had occurred. (2) Dr. Yerington confirmed that the conversations had happened during a period when Frank's EEG was isoelectric (flatline EEG). It was not possible for him to have heard these conversations. Most astonishing of all was the fact that when Dr. Yerington checked, the serial numbers were correct.

FLAPPING SURGEON

In this case, a patient reported seeing an unusual activity while having an OBE.

Circumstances: Al Sullivan was undergoing surgery due to a heart problem in Hartford Hospital, USA. During the surgery, he had an OBE.

The two criteria were met as follows: (1) As soon as Mr Sullivan was able to speak, he told his cardiologist, Dr. Anthony LaSala, about his OBE in which he saw a doctor standing over his body flapping his arms as though he were trying to take off. (2) Dr. LaSala was taken aback by this account as Mr Sullivan's eyes had been taped shut during the operation. There was also a drape between the patient's head and the open chest cavity in which the surgeon was operating. Also, given the stage of the operation where Sullivan noted the arm flapping, he was almost certainly unconscious. The surgeon, Hiroyoshi Takata, was known for using his elbows to gesture to others what he wanted to do and held his arms like wings when he did so. Takata, who seemed a bit defensive about the observations by the patient, would not confirm whether or not he did this during Mr Sullivan's operation but said it was something he did routinely. Other details Sullivan reported were confirmed by Dr. LaSala, and were things Sullivan could not possibly have known.

MARIA'S TENNIS SHOE

This is probably the most famous verified OBE, as it was one of the first to be publicly discussed and presented by Kenneth Ring, one of the founding fathers of NDE research. This occurred in 1979 in a Harbourview Hospital in Seattle, USA.

Circumstances: Maria, a Spanish-speaking migrant worker, had a CA after being admitted into hospital a couple of days earlier.

Maria reported details from her OBE that fulfil the two criteria: (1) She told a social worker in the hospital, Kimberly Clark Sharp, about her OBE, and asked Sharp to see if there was a blue tennis shoe on a window ledge of the hospital a few floors off the ground. (2) Sharp investigated and found the shoe exactly how Maria described it. The social worker concluded that the only way Maria could have seen this was if she had indeed had an OBE. Various attempts to debunk this account have been made over the years, but none really hold water and say more about the character of the accusers than of the people involved.

THE 1985 QUARTER

Circumstances: An 82-year-old patient called Ricardo was admitted to a hospital in San Antonio, Texas, after collapsing. He had a CA in hospital but responded to resuscitation by Dr. John Lerma.

Once he was stabilized and fully conscious in the ICU, he was very eager to talk to Dr. Lerma about his OBE, and to confirm to himself that it had been real: (1) Ricardo relayed to the doctor various aspects of his NDE and OBE and said there was a 1985 quarter covered in dust on the top of a high cabinet in the trauma room. He asked Lerma to check if it was there, as he wanted to know whether the amazing experience, including the beautiful aspects of his NDE, were indeed real. (2) Dr. Lerma, in the presence of a couple of nurses, got a ladder and looked on top of the cabinet and found the dusty quarter, which was indeed dated 1985. This experience had such an impact on Dr. Lerma that he chose to pursue a career in end-of-life hospice medicine!

ANOTHER SERIAL NUMBER

Circumstances: At a hospital in New Jersey, a patient was admitted to a neurological unit in a coma. During her time there, she had a CA and was resuscitated.

When the patient came out of her coma, she told a nurse that she had had both an NDE and an OBE: (1) The patient told nurse Norma Bowe, who is now a PhD professor at Kean University, USA, that she had OCD with a fixation for remembering numbers, and that she had memorized the serial number on top of a 7-foot respirator that stood by her bed. Nurse Bowe made a note of the serial number. (2) A few days later, a technician came to remove the respirator because it was no longer needed. The nurse asked the technician to check if there was a serial number on the top. He did and it matched the number the patient had given.

WHEN IS ENOUGH ENOUGH?

There are more of these accounts—so many more that endless books are filled with them. I have chosen the above seven because they share similar characteristics; namely, the two criteria: (1) a patient reporting seeing something specific during an OBE and (2) an HCP confirming what was observed and, ideally, saying it was impossible for the patient to have made the observations through natural means.

What is so different regarding these seven cases (along with hundreds of other similar ones) and the following?

Circumstances: A patient was admitted to New York Langone Medical Center after collapsing with chest pain while shopping. The patient had a CA but was resuscitated and made a full recovery.

Two weeks later the patient was contacted by a researcher at the hospital, who asked if she had had any experiences before being resuscitated: (1) The patient said she had, but felt embarrassed about sharing them with the doctors, who were very busy—she remembered something she had seen while having an OBE. She had been above her body as the medical staff worked to resuscitate her and saw a screen facing the ceiling with a picture of a banana on it. (2) The researcher returned to Langone Medical Center, where he reported the patient interview to the research team. He did not know what had been projected at the time, but checked the time of the CPR on this patient and what the iPad was supposedly showing on the screen. It was indeed a banana.

Again, I ask what is so different between this and the seven cases described above? This case would obviously be one that might eventually occur and be reported within the AWARE II study and be called scientifically verified. Other than being part of a prospective study, in which the patients and staff were formally blinded to what the objects might be, this is essentially the same as the seven cases described. A patient reports to an HCP seeing something specific and verifiable during an OBE, the HCP checks that the observation was correct and that there is no way the patient could have seen this naturally. A banana on an iPad, a quarter on a cupboard, a serial number on a light, there is no difference. Both forms of evidence are empirical and are equally valid - one being the observational evidence from scientific experts, the other a report from an experiment.

The real issue here is that the wider academic community, which is strongly attached to a materialistic worldview, chooses to suggest that the highly trained HCPs with careers in medicine were either fools or liars. I prefer to look at the facts, which are as follows:

- Thousands of OBEs have been reported over the years.
- The vast majority of these OBEs were reported by ordinary people who had just experienced severe trauma, and had nothing to gain from sharing what they believe had happened to them (as evidenced by the fact that their details are often not shared). To suggest that these thousands of patients imagined accurate details or were masters of illusion that make the magicians Penn and Teller look like amateurs is absurd.
- Many hundreds of OBEs have been verified by highly professional HCPs, and sometimes by preeminent physicians who have been leaders in their field.
- These HCPs are often skeptical by nature—to suggest they were so easily fooled is an insult to their considerable intelligence, training, and professionalism. Such suggestions tell us more about the person making the suggestion than about anything else.
- The only alternative is that hundreds of HCPs across the world decided to lie in order to propagate a belief that the consciousness is able to survive death.

The fact is that it requires either a huge leap of imagination/delusion or a degree of materialistic stubbornness, which makes a mule look compliant, to believe that either of the last two explanations is remotely plausible.

If you add in the sum total of evidence supporting the case for OBEs being real, and no evidence against them being real, then it becomes far more rational to understand that the consciousness is a separate entity from the brain and survives death.

Skeptics argue that we need more data. What they are really saying is that they need scientifically verified data because they do not want to believe the empirical evidence provided by thousands of doctors. We already have sufficient data. We have thousands of verified anecdotal reports of OBEs from credible humans, including healthcare professionals. We also have two verified reports of OBEs observed by research scientists in professional research settings.

I do not know about you, but an iPad telling me it happened is not going to make it any more compelling. I have shown above that we have enough evidence now to make an informed decision—OBEs have been proven beyond reasonable doubt to be a real phenomenon.

This has implications. If the OBE element of an NDE is proven real, then surely all the other elements – tunnel, dead relatives, Being of Light etc - are also proven real? This was certainly my thinking until recently, but there has been a subtle shift in how I see things.

CHAPTER 5: WHAT DO THE NDE RESULTS MEAN?

Having reached our first destination of learning that the evidence proves OBEs are real, the gates are now open to a whole realm of implied possibilities. We will now travel through that realm, considering each of these possibilities in turn.

What does this proof of the reality of OBEs mean for humanity, and in particular the existence of the eternal soul?

It means everything.

THE EXISTENCE OF THE ETERNAL SOUL

It is important to note that while the data we have all but proves the existence of a soul that is able to separate from the body, it does not prove the existence of a soul that persists eternally, something I touched on in the introduction.

At this point I am going to very briefly fulfil my promise of addressing the theological debate that has existed since shortly after the church formed—the debate between those Christians who adhere to the idea that the soul is eternal and inhabits a mortal body versus those who believe that our soul and body are one entity and that Christians will see their physical bodies resurrected on the "last day." This, after all, is what Jesus seemed to suggest in John 5:28–29 and John 6:44. You could write a whole book on this topic, but for me it is very much a side issue.

The Bible does not reveal all knowledge on every subject except for the character and nature of God, and what he require of us. The Bible provides clues to the answers to many of man's deepest questions, but also allows a degree of freedom to speculate on the exact nature of life, the universe, and everything as new evidence emerges. As Paul says in 1 Corinthians 13, "For now we see only a reflection as in a mirror; then we shall see face to face. Now I know in part; then I shall know fully, even as I am fully known." For instance, take the fact that the earth goes around the sun. Today, only a few crazy people believe this is not true, and yet until Copernicus and Galileo proved the opposite, the church taught that the earth is the static center of the universe as fact based on verses from Joshua 10 and 2 Kings 20. At the time there were theologians who regarded Galileo's declarations as heretical, and he was held under house arrest for years by the Vatican because of it. The church has repeated this type of mistake numerous times since and some Christians may do so again when we are given what could be argued is the most substantial piece of evidence from human experience supporting religious faith that has ever existed. Once again, the church could "drop the ball" and blow an amazing opportunity to lead millions of curious minds to the foot of the cross.

Now we have evidence, which I would argue is proof beyond reasonable doubt, that, for some people, and for a short time at least, the soul leaves the earthly physical body when that body clinically dies. Does this therefore contradict what Jesus said in the Gospel of John? No. We don't know what happens after that…a very important point that I will discuss later. According to the Bible there will be a new heaven and new earth (Revelations 21), with new heavenly bodies (2 Corinthians 5:1-6). Do we come back after a stint in heaven? Do some stay in heaven, and some come back? Do we sleep? Do we never leave our bodies, and these OBEs are just clever illusions? I have discussed this with several Bible-believing, Jesus-loving Christians, including the copy editor of this book, and each has come up with a completely different answer! I do not have the answer. As a scientist I could speculate on a quantum mechanical explanation of the soul and body being separated but still connected across time and space, but I would not have a clue what I was talking about, so won't, and frankly it appears that theologians can't quite agree on this either. Paul's description of "heavenly bodies: we will not be spirits without bodies" in 2 Corinthians 5 is uncanny in the similarities of reports from NDEs. I lean towards that understanding.

Christians need to pick their fights more wisely, and I do not believe fighting for a particular understanding of precisely what happens to our bodies at the end of times is a hill worth dying on. Many Christians have turned curious minds away from seeking Jesus by clinging to and promoting pet theological positions which seem esoteric to everyone else. Will someone's eternal destiny be decided by what they believe on the issue of human physical resurrection? I doubt it. However, there are hills worth dying on, for instance that Jesus' body was physically resurrected—the tomb really was empty in that instance, and believing that is central to Christian faith, something I will discuss later.

From this point on, much of the hypothesizing I engage in is based on the understanding that at least for the duration of NDEs, the soul leaves its earthly body during clinical death. The specific mechanics of what happens to our souls and bodies in the case of real death I will leave to the theologians to argue about, but please don't do it in front of unbelievers. Now let us return to the main discussion.

The conclusions drawn from the data on validated NDEs relate only to the period of time that the patient was clinically dead. The studies do not and cannot prove anything beyond that. However, I will hypothesize on what the data infers regarding the existence of an eternal soul. This discussion will have both evidence-based and philosophical elements to it.

Some may argue that this "floating" consciousness is some sort of quantum hangover from the brain's life and would stop existing at some point, but that is pure speculation with no evidence to support it. It may be true that the mechanisms of consciousness are somehow connected to quantum mechanics—for example, subatomic processes may enable the consciousness to exist in and interact with the tangible physical dimension—but that provides no evidence pointing to the origin of this consciousness or its ability to persist indefinitely. If the consciousness uses quantum level processes to interact with the brain, it does not necessarily imply that the brain generates this consciousness.

The evidence for the belief that consciousness persists much longer than the duration of the NDE does not lie in science but rather in the thousands of different belief systems that have evolved over the millennia that state the soul is eternal. Various prophets have said so in one form or another, some of whom were very specific about the eternal nature of a person's soul. Jesus also taught this. Many tribal belief systems maintain that their ancestors exist as "spirits." In addition, some NDErs report that they are told by beings they meet during their NDEs that the soul is eternal and will persist forever.

In isolation, these pieces of "evidence" do not amount to anything more than subjective beliefs, but when combined with the clear proof that the consciousness is independent of the body and is able to exist beyond death, these subjective reports and "understandings" need to be taken more seriously. They both corroborate and are corroborated by the totality of data from validated OBEs. It is now rational to believe that our consciousness has the potential to be eternal.

This is the first and most important "so what" to come out of the findings of the AWARE studies.

However, that is just the beginning since if OBEs are proven to be real, then surely by extrapolation so too are other core elements of NDEs. That seems to make sense, and it did for a long time to me, but having read and watched hundreds, if not thousands, of accounts, my answer has become more nuanced.

OBEs are objectively measurable—there is nothing subjective about a serial number. However, as we will see, most of the core elements of NDEs—the elements consistently reported by NDErs—are impossible to test objectively. They appear, at the very least, subjective in their observations and sometimes even contradictory, as we will discover.

Does this mean that the subjective parts, or other core elements of the NDE experience, are not real? I believe they are no more or less real than the world we experience; in fact, NDErs often describe the experience as more real. However, I believe this latter observation is related to the state that they are in; namely, the unrestrained nature of their consciousness when released from their bodies, rather than the place they are in. It is this state of being that creates the sense of greater "realness" rather than the nature of the realms and events they witness. Their senses of what they experience are magnified, leading them to state that things feel more real. But does this mean that what they report is a complete and accurate report of what lies beyond life?

I once said yes, but now say that the reports are of experiences within a spiritual dimension impossible for us to fully identify or understand. I am no longer certain that what people report to be heaven, is actually God's heaven—or at least the complete version of it. Before we get into why my view has shifted to that position, let us go through the core elements of an NDE other than an OBE.

THE OTHER CORE ELEMENTS

It could be argued that if the other core elements of an NDE were generated by chemical or electrical events in a dying brain or from experiencing pulses of oxygenated blood via CPR, then they should be much more random in nature. While there are subtle, and sometimes important, differences between individual accounts, the central aspects of each element are reproducible across all demographics. Moreover, the sequence of events reported in NDEs always seems to follow a logical and consistent timeline, or narrative arc. This internal consistency points to these experiences being "real" in that NDErs did indeed experience these events while their brains were not working.

So, what are these other core elements?

They are the other nine components of the Greyson scale for measuring whether conscious recollections reported from CA survivors are classified as NDEs or not:

1. Awareness of being dead.
2. Intense emotions, most commonly of profound peace, well-being, and love; others marked by fear, horror, and loss.
3. Rapidly moving through darkness or a tunnel, often toward an indescribable light.
4. Incredibly fast, sharp thoughts and observations.
5. A sense of being "somewhere else," in a landscape that seems like a spiritual realm or world (I prefer to use the word "dimension").
6. Encounter with deceased loved ones, sacred figures or unrecognized beings who are consoling, loving, or terrifying.

7. A life review by reliving actions and feeling their emotional impact on others.
8. A boundary that represents a decision to return to the body or to stay.
9. Communication with a supreme Being of Light, or just light.

Let us break these down for a brief closer look.

AWARENESS OF BEING DEAD

This is self-explanatory and is not really subjective. People having an OBE with an awareness of being dead often describe looking at their dead body and feeling nothing. Occasionally they may be sad or afraid, but the most common emotional response to the sight of their dead bodies is indifference. Perhaps if we fully internalized the truth that our consciousness survived beyond the death of our earthly bodies, we might not think that the death of our bodies is as horrible as we believe it to be while physically alive. Our desperate need to cling to physical life might, for a moment, be removed and our earthly body might become almost anachronistic, even an encumbrance. Many describe the return to their bodies as unpleasant, confining, and even disappointing.

INTENSE EMOTIONS

Once the consciousness has left their body, some people report feeling intense emotions. The one most often described is an overwhelming sense of peace, an assurance that everything will be all right. Also, people report experiencing love with an intensity greater than they ever experienced in this life. Others, thankfully in the minority, have extremely negative emotions marked by fear or even horror.

Here we see a divergence between accounts. For those who have peaceful sensations, they will often speak in a way that this is the outcome for everyone. That it is the destiny for all humanity—universalism. Some claim that is what they are told by "spirit guides," but how can that be true if other NDErs report the opposite sensation?

The common element is that they experience emotions that are very intense. Those who experience peace are filled head to toe with it, but those who experience fear and horror are equally filled with these extremely negative emotions. The interpretations of these experiences are very different and form the subjective element of NDE accounts.

RAPIDLY MOVING THROUGH DARKNESS OR A TUNNEL

After an OBE, many NDErs describe passing through a tunnel of some sort, often at an incredible speed and accompanied by the sound of wind and the sense of passing through time and space. Often there is a light at the end of the tunnel—a light they are drawn to.

I will not go into discussions often cited about physiological explanations of the tunnel involving the last signals from the retina. Right now, we are working on the assumption that because the OBE has been proven to be real, all other reports of core elements by extrapolation are reports of events that occurred while the patient was clinically dead.

So, what does this tunnel represent? Since it often precedes NDErs having experiences of other dimensions, good and bad, it would not be unreasonable to believe this is a passage between the universe in which we live—one that is dominated by the rules of physics and time—and somewhere else. Or perhaps it could be a connection to another place within this universe (although people often describe being outside time). Either is complete conjecture, but it is reported as a journey of immeasurable length and time, as though there is a clear demarcation between two different dimensions.

Again, when this element is reported, while the overarching themes of moving rapidly through space and time are consistent, the observations are not. Some will say it is a tunnel; others, something different. Some say it is dark; others, many different colours. Some do not go through anything and end up suspended in outer space as an orb of light! However, to each of these NDErs the experience felt real and that their consciousness had expanded.

INCREDIBLY RAPID, SHARP THOUGHTS AND OBSERVATIONS

In OBEs, on both sides of the "tunnel," people often describe all their senses as being enhanced. For example, they describe having 360-degree vision. They are able to perceive new colours that were not visible before. Also, their speed of understanding and other aspects of cognition are accelerated. Answers to deep mysteries are suddenly understood with no effort of thought.

Many take on a physical but complete or enhanced version of their former bodies. One of the most remarkable types of reports is of NDErs who are blind from birth in this life but once released from their bodies see for the first time. These accounts are compelling.

However, as I said in the previous section, not everyone seems to take on the form of a human body. Some feel absorbed into a greater "universal or corporate" consciousness, or become floating orbs of light, among other things.

So once again there is a commonality of NDErs saying that senses and cognition are hugely heightened but there is not absolute consistency regarding the characteristics between their reported states. A key difference is between whether they retain a unique identity and sense of individual "physical" form, or become part of a greater "oneness", without familiar physical form, but still retain an awareness of being unique. Again, all NDErs will say we are one with everyone and everything around us, but the understanding of the delineation of where this oneness starts and the individual ends is different, and sometimes so markedly different that it is not possible to interpret this just as differing recollections of the same thing. They are experiencing something different that results in their returning with contradicting understandings of the nature of our selves beyond death. Does this mean their experiences are not real?

Again, I will return to the analogy of dreams. While experiencing dreams, they feel real, even if they are bizarre, but the moment we awake we know they were not real. I had a dream last night during which I drank a coffee. I can remember actually tasting the coffee! It felt real, but I know now it was a dream.

When people return from their NDEs, they are adamant their experiences were very different from dreams, and felt more real than this world—but then how do you explain these discrepancies? My stab at an answer would be something along the lines that dream worlds and "NDE worlds" are very different in nature, but that allowing our understanding of "reality" to be flexed will help us glimpse possible answers to this puzzle. I will explore what I think may be going on once we get to the end of this chapter.

A SENSE OF BEING "SOMEWHERE ELSE"

In my father's NDE, he found himself in a meadow surrounded by flowers that were beautiful beyond imagination with colors he had never before seen. This is a quite common report from NDEs. People from a Christian Western culture will usually describe this "realm" as heaven, but is it?

Many Christians, as I did for a long time, latch on to this as proof that heaven exists. As I have been saying, my position on this has shifted.

While NDErs describe these experiences as being beyond the ability of human terminology to express, it is also true to say that no single subjective account of the landscapes, forms, buildings, or vistas observed in these realms is the same as another—especially when you look at NDEs from different cultures. There is huge variability and, while they all describe these places as feeling more real than life here and as being their real home, the fact they are all different leaves some unanswered questions. Surely God's heaven is consistent and does not shift in its appearance or content from one person's visit to the next? Again, I do not question the authenticity of all the accounts, or the report that the experience felt more real than "real life," but the lack of consistency must give pause for thought. It must also be noted, though, at this point that at least some of the NDE stories are fabricated. In 2015, Alex Malarkey—a boy with a story of visiting heaven during an NDE—publicly recanted his own story and book *The Boy Who Came Back from Heaven*, by Alex and Kevin Malarkey, stating that his near death experience described in that book was fictional, and condemned Christian publishers and bookstores for selling popular "heaven tourism" books, which he said "profit from lies." I do not believe all NDEs are fabricated, but some must be. How do we tell which ones?

As for the consistencies, there are sometimes cities and buildings in these experiences. Some describe a library with the books of life in it (but the layout or structure is different in different experiences). There are often beautiful scenes of lakes, mountains, beaches, fields, gardens, and so on, often described as what we imagine heaven to be but infinitely better. In addition, we are told there is access to unlimited knowledge, although when people come back they have forgotten most of that knowledge! NDErs invariably meet "angels" or "spirit guides" who tell them the meaning of life and to return and live their lives accordingly. Sometimes they meet a supreme Being of Light often described as God—we will come to that in its own section. These are all commonalities that are frequently repeated, but the descriptions are often markedly different, pointing to two possible scenarios:

1. The NDErs are seeing exactly the same thing but applying subjective interpretation in their memories, which seems unlikely given the degree of inconsistency in specifics.
2. They are having a "tailored" experience, designed and created for each individual.

Both scenarios suggest an incomplete, or in a worst-case scenario, a false or misleading picture. I am not saying that the NDEr is always behind any falsehood, but if not the NDEr, then what or who?

Ultimately, my position on whether this is "a" heaven or "the" heaven—especially in light of the inconsistencies I have come to be aware of reading so many accounts—has defaulted to what Jesus says on this subject, and he does have a very specific message. I will come to that later when we measure NDE accounts against the Gospels, but for now consider what Paul said in 2 Corinthians 12:2, "I know a man in Christ who fourteen years ago was caught up to the third heaven. Whether it was in the body or out of the body I do not know—God knows." In the context of this book, his use of the expression "out of the body" is striking. I will shortly share my own experience that is a faint echo of that which the great apostle seemed to have, but nonetheless has had a profound impact on my life. It is in fact one of the "foundations" of my faith and why, if there is any doubt, my default is always Jesus.

In concluding this topic, I have no doubt that this place is a spiritual realm authentically experienced by the souls of the clinically dead but due to the lack of consistency in the descriptions, and some important details, we must ask the question "Is this place the heaven and if not, what is it?" I will come back to this.

There is of course another spiritual realm talked about in the Bible and other religious texts: hell. Is there evidence for this from NDEs?

According to historical accounts between 6 and 25% of reported NDEs describe going down a different road than the one that leads to a beautiful spiritual realm. As is the case with all NDEs, these darker experiences may differ in specific details, but usually share certain themes or elements.

In the recent 2022 consensus statement[2] created by Dr. Sam Parnia and other leading NDE researchers that I mentioned earlier, these experiences have been dismissed as not being true NDEs. Specifically, in the supplemental section the following statement is made:

> However, typically, these so called "negative NDEs" neither share the same narrative nor themes as the classical NDE, nor do they share the same transcendent qualities, ineffability, and long-term transformative effects of the classical NDE. *In sum, so called negative NDEs appear to be fundamentally and phenomenologically different from the classical NDE.* In reality, the majority of these descriptions largely represent a mislabelling of ICU delirium and delusions . . . (my italics)

This statement has a single citation attached to it.[15] This Cassol et al. paper, the source used by the consensus panel to formulate its position, repeats a number of times that the only overall difference in terms of measurable elements of negative NDEs from classical NDEs is that negative NDEs result in a less positive affect, and "distressing and classical accounts do not seem to differ regarding total score as well as on the three other components of the Greyson NDE scale (i.e. cognitive, paranormal and transcendental)." And, "Finally, memories of distressing NDEs appear as phenomenologically detailed as classical ones." And:

> Regarding our last aim [the phenomenological and contextual differences existing between the memories of distressing and classical NDEs], distressing and classical NDEs were found to have comparable total scores on the Greyson NDE scale. A detailed analysis revealed that these two types of experiences only differed on

the affective subscale. Those findings were expected since three items clearly stipulate the presence of positively connoted emotions.[15]

In other words, due to the fact that the Greyson scale focuses on positive feelings, the only difference between negative and positive NDEs was the level of positive feelings. Not really surprising given what these poor souls had been through. As a reader, and possibly one who would normally trust scientists and physicians to "get things right," it is really helpful for you to see this kind of extreme "confirmation bias" in action (so extreme that Parnia takes a piece of evidence 100% against the position he is supporting and presents it as evidence for it!). As a scientist who has been writing in Christian apologetics, I am unfortunately all too familiar with this. It would almost be funny if the subject were not so utterly serious and the consequences of getting this wrong so eternally devastating. Sam Parnia, professor of emergency medicine, is one of the world's leading researchers on this topic. He is regularly quoted in newspapers and seen on TV talking about it, and is familiar with all the evidence regarding NDEs. Parnia has stuck his academic neck out by repeatedly going on the record saying NDEs are real, yet cannot countenance the idea that hell exists. His bias is so blind, his well-meaning desire for nothing so terrible to happen to anyone so strong, that he reads black as white, and up as down and then makes it a guideline for future research to never mention these experiences again. Now that really is confirmation bias!

In the Cassol et al. paper, 14% of people have negative NDEs, about half of whom have hellish NDEs, and the descriptions bare many similarities to classical NDEs, such as a tunnel, being hyper aware, timelessness, OBEs, 360-degree vision. Parnia's position may be well meaning but, as I said earlier, the well-worn phrase "The path to hell is paved with good intentions" could not be more appropriate. Anyway, I hope you understand my frustration with this. Let us move on.

One common theme in these hellish experiences is the presence of other extremely unpleasant beings. In Howard Storm's account of his NDE in the book, My Descent Into Death, he describes popping out of his body, and after frantically trying to get his wife to listen to him, but to no avail, he heard voices coming from beyond an open door in the corner of the hospital room. He decided to follow them since initially the voices surrounding him seemed friendly. But suddenly their demeanour changed, and even though he no longer had an earthly physical body, they began to violate him. The pain felt real, and the fear was absolute. Fortunately, he escaped. Were those beings demons or tortured souls?

It is impossible to know, but there are many other accounts of people experiencing pain and suffering in their NDE and returning from the experience with a real fear of death. It is also possible this type of NDE is underreported because the people were ashamed, embarrassed, confused, or simply thought it was a form of nightmare. There is also another potential explanation related to memory that I discuss in a later section. Either way it poses a very important question: Is this place really hell?

This lady, whose experience is recounted in the 2019 Cassol et al. paper on negative NDEs, states that it is:

> There are more and more entities surrounding me and this dark environment is unbearable. The deafening noise invades the space that becomes increasingly dark. I would like this noise to stop. I am caught in a whirlwind, the dark grey haze around me is thick, and the smell and sound are getting more unbearable [. . .]. And I am beginning to distinguish forms in this incredibly thick fog. Human, bestial, monstrous. I am swimming in a stinking stench filled with horrible and furtive creatures and I am feeling overwhelmed with pain. It hurts everywhere, no, worse, I am becoming pain. I understand that my suffering is just beginning. And I am scared.

A growing fear, appalling. I would like to close my eyes and stop hearing and feeling. But it is impossible. My vision is very wide, I see everywhere at once, I see in front of me, above, below and on the sides; only a small part on the back is not visible. The less I want to hear, see and feel, the more receptive I am. It is terrible, it is like I am absorbing the pain and suffering of all these beings . . . I am extremely lucid, I feel aware like I have never been before. Time no longer exists. I wish I could escape this place, escape time, but my anguish is such that I cannot move . . . as if these beings were holding me back. [. . .] I understand that I am between two worlds and that this in-between is none other than Hell. (Female, 42 years old)

Accounts like this should not be dismissed as readily as Dr. Parnia does and should serve as warnings that eternal joy is not guaranteed, as some of the universalists suggest. The strangest thing of all about Parnia's stance is that in his latest book, Lucid Dying, he uses the account of a woman who (unsuccessfully) committed suicide, and who witnessed a hellish scene in her NDE, to warn against attempting suicide. In other words, despite on the one hand dismissing hell-like experiences as ICU delirium, on the other he accepts an account with a hell-like scene in it as authentic.

Another common dark theme reported by many NDErs is precisely that, an experience of darkness. Not just any darkness, but a creeping, cold darkness that threatens to engulf them and from which they know there is no return. Is this hell or is it ultimate death—that is, the death of the soul—a topic to which I will return later?

Are these dark experiences completely random, or is there some correlation between faith in God and/or "righteous" behavior in this life? There is very little available from the accounts to steer our thinking on this. Some who have had these dark experiences said they believed in God, and some who claim to have good experiences were atheists (though they rarely are afterwards).

The answers are not easily discerned from the accounts, and I personally fall back on what my faith tells me about this subject. Others may be left somewhat baffled by it.

Also, I think it is worth applying the same approach to the "heavenly" realms that I did above. Is this really hell, or is it something else, another spiritual realm people describe as hell? Who knows?

According to some NDE reports, it is possible that the dark state we describe as hell is not necessarily eternal. Howard Storm's experience was not permanent: he is one of many who report escaping a state of torment and entering a heavenly realm. His route is one I have heard a number of times in NDE accounts and involved calling out to Jesus for help.

Even though Howard Storm and others returned to life from their NDEs, one cannot help but ask what happens to those who enter the dark state and stay dead? Is it different for them? Can they escape it? These reports may give us glimpses of truths, but they also raise more questions than they answer.

Finally, regarding the different realms, some NDErs report entering a state of limbo where they experience a "restless state of greyness."

ENCOUNTER WITH DECEASED LOVED ONES, SACRED FIGURES, OR UNRECOGNIZED BEINGS

Many NDErs describe meeting relatives or occasionally friends (and even pets) whom they were close to during their lives. The NDErs are often welcomed. Sometimes they sense others whom they did not know. They are described as guardian angels or "spirit guides." This has often been reported in accounts by reliable NDErs. What the spirit guides are and what role they have is completely open to interpretation. While there is strong correlation across different incidences, the perceptions and understandings of what the NDErs experience are subjective.

The Bible advises us in this life, while we are still in the physical dimension, not to dabble with mediums, and so on, and not try speaking to the dead. However, given that these people are dead, and such communication happens, it is hard to know what to think of it. I return to my thoughts on spirit guides, and so on, later when cross-referencing with the Gospels.

A LIFE REVIEW

Countless NDErs report the experience of seeing their whole life, every minute detail, and being invited to reflect on all their actions and the impacts those actions had on those around them. It is an "objective" analysis guided by a "celestial" being, or beings, covering what went well and what did not. They also get to experience their behavior from other people's viewpoints, specifically to show how their actions made others feel.

Almost as an aside, I want to mention again my favorite NDE account, that of Howard Storm who experienced a remarkable NDE that turned his life in a completely different direction—a reasonably common outcome. He went from being an atheist Christian-bashing university professor to a Baptist minister. His NDE is famous for many things, some of which I will return to, but what really struck me was his account of his life review. Howard Storm had been an academic and an accomplished sportsman. He had obviously been someone driven to succeed, but when he experienced his life review with "other beings," the piece of his life they got the most excited about—and which got the highest "approval ratings"—was the night when, as a teenager, he heard his sister crying in a neighboring bedroom and went in to hug and comfort her for the rest of the night. This appeared to be one of the most important things he did in his entire life.

This points to a common component that comes from virtually all NDEs: life is about many things, but most of all it is about loving others.

According to many NDErs, our primary purpose in life is to love. I will come back to this aspect, regarded as the central teaching of NDErs, later. I know some astute Christians will already have alarm bells ringing loudly in their ears!

Another aspect of the life review is that those who experience it rarely describe it as judgment. It is more a review of how you behaved surrounded by a loving nurturing group of spiritual beings. You do feel ashamed of the things you did that were wrong, but you are not judged for them by others. You do, however, get to see every ripple of negativity that your slightest misplaced word caused, and yet you are not invited to seek forgiveness. It is all about learning—another central teaching of the NDE "religion."

Some will argue that this shows that there is no judgment for humanity. In my view, this core element, which is frequently reported, provides no evidence whatsoever as to whether or not there is a judgment for all when they die. Again, more on this later. However, there is an oft-overlooked core element, mentioned in passing, that has become central to the rationale for my shifting my view on many of the issues we have begun to discuss.

A BOUNDARY

Many NDErs report a point in their experience where they are told, or are aware, that if they go any farther into this new dimension, they can never come back. Alternatively, sometimes, even if they want to stay—as is often the case because the experience can be beautiful—they are told they cannot go beyond the boundary and must return, as they have not completed their purpose in life.

Previously, that was all I said on this core element but, like everyone else, I was missing the huge significance of this boundary and its implications. When considering all the reports NDErs come back with, we must at all times remember this central fact: they came back, they did not stay dead.

They did not experience death as we understand it to be—permanent. They nearly died.

Had they crossed the boundary, and forever left this life, what would they have seen? Would they have been judged? Would a different heaven (or hell) await? We will never know in this life, and I have come to see that this core element is hugely significant and one that means we must view all other subjective aspects of the experience, all the varying accounts, in the following light: NDEs are at the very best an incomplete picture of what awaits us after death.

To view them any other way is to ignore the fact that so many report this boundary exists. Why would there be a boundary if it were not for the possibility that further revelations and truths lie beyond, ones that must forever stay beyond the boundary of mortal human knowledge? Moreover, this boundary relates to a specific word from Jesus, which I alluded to earlier, and will return to in the chapter where I measure NDE accounts against the Gospels.

Now we come to the last and possibly the most important core element: communication with a supreme Being of Light, or just light.

COMMUNICATION WITH A SUPREME BEING

> ...the NDE evidence implies that a supreme being exists whose essence is love and light. Testimony after testimony describes near-death individuals meeting a divine being of light before whom they experienced nothing but unconditional love and acceptance. This is, in fact, among the most consistent elements of western NDEs from the earliest studies through the present day.[16]

The above is a quote from one of many websites on NDEs and expresses a common theme: in spite of cultural interpretations of who the being is, the

Being of Light is universally described as a being of immense loving power.

In my previous book, I stated that this must be God. I argued that along with other evidence we have through science and human testimony, this provides conclusive evidence that God exists. One of the reasons I adopted this position over the years is that there was commonality with my own "transcendental" experience, which I will now share with you.

When I was a teenager, I was a "nominal" Christian—Christian in name only. I had some belief in God, in Jesus, but like many of my generation in the eighties in the UK I saw Jesus as one of many ways to God, and my beliefs were all over the place. I did not have a personal relationship with God through faith in what Jesus said and did. When I was 17 my best friend invited me to a Christian retreat for teens. The basis for our wanting to attend was that there would be lots of "desperate" girls! I went and was disappointed not to be swamped by the advances of these girls. At the end of the weekend there was a service and a call for those who had not yet given their lives to Christ to say the prayer of repentance, which goes something like this: "Lord Jesus I am sorry I have not fully recognized you as Lord; I am sorry for all the things I have done wrong. Please forgive me for the things I have done wrong and for ignoring you. Please save me, please come into my life and become my Lord."

I felt something spiritual tugging me towards the front to say this prayer. However, I still had other plans, which as a teen involved partying hard, finding girls who would accept my advances, becoming a pop star or England cricket batsmen or wealthy businessman, and so on, and the last thing I wanted was for the Christian faith to hold me back from my worldly ambitions. I rejected the only advances I received that weekend—the ones from God.

About six months later, during which time I had still not had much luck with girls, was not a pop star, and had dropped out of the village cricket side due to my hard partying, I had my experience.

I had been asleep, but awoke in the middle of the night. My room was exactly how it was when I went to sleep. Everything felt very normal, real, not dreamlike, but I felt compelled to get out of bed, get down on my knees and say the prayer I had avoided saying that weekend.

I can remember my elbows sinking into the bean bag I was resting on as I said the words, but the moment I finished the prayer—boom!

The room literally disintegrated into a trillion pieces and I was somewhere else. It was pitch dark, but I was not alone or afraid. I sensed I was in a great hall and there were many people around me; then, all of a sudden, only one took my attention. I could not see this being, but it connected with me and lavished unbelievable indescribable love on me. It was like every single particle of my being was on fire with a love like I had never known in this life; I was loved and loved back with all-consuming intensity. It felt like the wildest romantic love, but without the sexuality, and completely fulfilled me. If it had lasted forever, it would not have been long enough.

Then I awoke in my bed. Was it just a dream? Normally when I "wake up" in a dream, things are far from normal. But in this dream, it felt exactly the same as if I had actually awoken in "real" life.

Did I become a Christian at that point?

No! God might have blessed me with a good scientific brain; but when it comes to other things, I can be remarkably stupid sometimes. It took another year of failed partying and God's pulling me into a family that loved Jesus, through a daughter who accepted my advances, to get me to the point that I was able to say that prayer and mean it.

I have no doubt that the experience I had was of God on the other side of the veil of our flesh through which we normally perceive things. Sometimes, I get glimpses of that in private prayer, and more often in corporate worship at the remarkable Chanctonbury Church I attend, but nothing so complete as in that experience. It was more real than anything I had experienced before. It was perfect. It is one of the pillars of my faith that allows not a scintilla of doubt to exist in my mind of the existence of God and his nature.

When I started reading about NDEs and people's encounters with the Being of Light, I heard the same kinds of words I have just used to describe my experience: their descriptions seemed both to corroborate and be corroborated by what happened to me. This is God.

Now I have some doubts whether they experienced the same God.

I am certain that what I experienced was indeed God. Christians reading this will understand that the route by which my experience happened was an "officially approved" route, for want of a better expression. But what about NDEr reports of the Being of Light?

For me, the Being of Light is the most significant subjective element of the NDE. This element, more than any other, can be the most transformative. It alters perspective forever and puts into context the daily squabbles over money, work, and power. After this encounter, the experiencer is left with no doubt that it is the Being of Light's desire for us to live our lives as loving beings. The message seems to be that there is never any excuse for taking another human life, especially for the sake of imposing a religion or ideology on others. In addition, the pursuit of material possessions, power, or recognition is a dangerous distraction from our primary purpose, which is to love. Feedback from NDErs who claim to have communicated with the Being of Light or other spiritual beings on the other side share a consistent message: life is about two things. First, and most importantly, it is about loving. Second, it is about learning. Some NDErs describe earth as a school, one of the toughest.

What is not to like? Surely this is what God wants? Surely this is God?

While the God I know wants these things, there is something he wants more than anything else, even more than all these wonderful noble things. It took me a long time to notice that the thing Christians are told God most wants is the thing that always seems to be missing from the list of commands NDErs come back with. Christians should know exactly what I am talking about. I will return to it later when I measure what NDErs say against the teachings of Jesus.

For now, though, I am on the fence regarding who this being from NDE reports is and I am not 100% convinced any more that it is the God I know, love, and trust. Please note, though, I am far from 100% convinced it is not either, and I doubt my position (or lack of it) will change in this lifetime—for reasons I will state later when we come to the final chapters.

CHAPTER 6: WHAT ABOUT THE TEN PERCENT?

I have kept this section separate as I believe it is one of the most important objective findings to come out of NDE research, and a subject that seems to be largely skimmed over by other writers. The possible conclusions I have drawn about this subject are not the same as the wider NDE community, who largely try to avoid anything negative. Again, which explanation you accept is a choice. However, I believe this issue provides strong evidence to support Jesus' teachings on the subject of our eternal destination, as we shall begin to see.

In this section I add a new word that can be interchanged with "soul" or "consciousness": *spirit*. This word has a religious association but describes the same entity I have been referring to throughout this book. Concepts such as spirituality are going to be covered in this section, and there are no equivalent words with the same meaning; it is necessary to introduce it.

I have described three types of realms or experiences reported from many NDEs: the dark hellish type, the light heavenly one, and the grey limbo type. But there is one more possible outcome: death. By that I do not mean physical death, but something I believe is far worse: spiritual death. Those familiar with the teachings of Jesus will know this (incomplete) verse: "Fear not the one who can kill your body, rather fear him who can kill your soul" (Matthew 10:28).

The idea of spiritual death—a concept embraced by some religions—is obviously entirely speculative in the context of the evidence we have been discussing. It is just one of a number of hypothetical explanations for the factual observation that not everyone who is clinically dead and then achieves ROSC has an NDE.

According to recent literature, cardiac arrests with reports of NDEs ranges somewhere between 10 and 20% of people, most of whom were elderly. It begs the question as to why everyone does not report NDEs, since we now know they are a real phenomenon.

Three possibilities come to mind:

1. 80–90% of people who have a CA do not report NDEs because, while they might have had one, they do not remember it.
2. 80–90% of times that people have a CA, the consciousness does not become immediately "detached" from the brain—it stays where it is in an unconscious state.
3. 80–90% of people who have a CA do not have an "eternal" soul or consciousness at the point of physical death—they have a consciousness suitable for existing in the physical world, but for some reason it is incapable of progressing to the "next dimension." One potential reason is that the part that was born eternal has become permanently "tethered" to the physical body that hosted it. Essentially, when the body dies, the soul will die with the flesh that hosts it.

Now let us break these down into more detail.

1. WHY WOULD SOMEONE HAVE AN NDE AND NOT REMEMBER IT?

It has been suggested that all people dream every night, but many people do not remember their dreams. Therefore, in the same way that people do not always remember their dreams, it may be possible that, for similar reasons, all people who have a CA also have an NDE, but not all people remember it.

This is perfectly plausible. It is certainly the explanation I believe to be most popular, as it is the least controversial or disquieting. Dr. Parnia once subscribed to this idea when presenting an explanation for this phenomenon. He now focuses on pharmacological and physiological reasons affecting memory. I still do not believe these reasons account for the 90%, though, not least because the data suggests that the brain is not working at all during these experiences. Therefore, these factors should not influence the laying down of memory. I will return to this very relevant detail at the end of this section.

Another physiological reason cited for not remembering NDEs has been covered previously and includes that the older the patient, the less likely they are to remember having one. This explanation may seem like common sense but, as I will discuss shortly, the data does not fully support this.

Another reason may be related to differing levels of innate spirituality. By this I mean that physiological or psychological factors may inhibit their ability to navigate, interact with, or, in this instance, remember events or encounters from this spiritual "dimension."

An example along these lines makes me think of a time when I began dating a woman who did not profess to have any faith but, because of mine, started attending church with me. However, even after a long period of attending together, our experiences of church and prayer were quite different. Sometimes, particularly in corporate worship songs, I experience a strong sense of "God's presence." However, she never had a sense of God's presence, despite our both being exposed to the possibility in an identical environment. She desperately wanted it and would pray for it, but to no avail.

What could be the reason?

- She was unable to experience the presence of God directly, despite seeking it, because she did not have the "natural" sensory capacity: her psychology or physiology did not allow it.
- She could not experience God's presence because God is a "spiritual" being and she did not have a sufficiently developed spirit/soul that was able to connect with or experience that dimension.

In other words, either her physical equipment (brain) was inadequate, or her consciousness was inadequate. So how could it be that one person has the natural sensory capacity in their brain to experience God and another does not?

During the early part of this century, researchers showed that spirituality may be a genetic trait. This evidence is discussed in Dean Hamer's book The God Gene, where he reviewed evidence that a portion of our genetic code called VMAT2 is related to our propensity to be spiritual.

What if a portion of the brain is like a radio receiver, capable of interacting with or sensing the presence of beings from the spiritual dimension, including a Being such as God? If that were true, and some people's brains were better developed in this area, then they might be more spiritual as a result. Conversely, if spiritual people were weeded out of society over the past hundreds of years through religious persecution, it is possible the VMAT2 gene has regressed and the general population has become less spiritual.

It is hard to see an evolutionary benefit to a spiritual gene if it does not deliver a physical survival advantage. Therefore, it should be equally present in—or absent from—all humans. However, while it may be true that being more spiritual does not lend a survival advantage (and in fact may be a disadvantage because of persecution), it is possible that being less spiritual does lend a survival advantage. If one's primary focus in life is on material gain and success, which are regarded as being less spiritual, it possibly confers a survival advantage to our material existence and therefore people with these traits become genetically dominant. This is of course a can of worms and is totally speculative, so not worth exploring further in this book.

In conclusion on spiritual ability, it may be possible that some people are less able to perceive spiritual things and yet still have a spirit. It is possible that despite people losing that connection between their physical minds and the spiritual world and becoming spiritually "blind," a soul or spirit still remains in that person. They may be isolated from the spiritual world and from God—which results in a lack of sensitivity in spiritual matters—but their status as spiritual beings is the same as those more developed spiritually.

Bringing this back to the subject at hand—memory of NDEs—a lack of spiritual awareness could also be linked to the ability to remember dreams or NDEs. The concepts may not seem connected, but all involve the consciousness either interacting with or existing in different (spiritual) dimensions—ones we now know to exist because OBEs have been proven real. It is possible that just as some people do not remember dreams or do not experience any spiritual presence, neither do they remember NDEs.

Another potential reason why people cannot remember NDEs may be due to the terrifying possibility that the experience was extremely traumatic. The specific term for this is dissociative amnesia. This can happen after a car accident, or from witnessing a murder, and so on. If, as mentioned previously, a small number of people report having a hell-like experience, maybe there are others for whom the experience was so horrific that their subconscious buried it (or would not access it) so they could not relive the trauma. Maybe hell-like NDEs are much more common than reported because some of those poor souls who have them cannot recall them due to dissociative amnesia.

I appreciate this is a very controversial and disturbing suggestion to those who are not Christians or are Christians who hold universalist beliefs, but nonetheless it should at least be considered a possibility. In fact, not to mention it would be a severe dereliction of my duty as a human being. Having read some of the "hellish" accounts and being familiar with warnings from various religions about the existence of hell, I want to do all in my power to stop a single soul experiencing such torment. I would rather include unpleasant truths in this book that cause it to be less popular, but steer people on to the right path, than ignore harsh realities to sell more copies. If I sell only one copy, which results in someone being "saved" from an experience so traumatic the brain stops your memory recalling it, then all the effort I have put into this project will be worthwhile.

Suffice to say, with our current level of knowledge, it is not possible to say with any certainty that people who have a CA and do not report NDEs are unable to report them because they do not remember them—either because they cannot form spiritual or dreamlike memories, or they simply struggle to remember in general, or they are suffering from dissociative amnesia.

Any of these explanations is potentially valid.

But putting them aside for a moment, there is an elephant in the room when it comes to the issue of remembering NDEs, which means this section should perhaps have been titled "Why would anyone remember an NDE?"

This points to the fact that not only does the brain have no ability to receive sensory information when someone is in a state of clinical death, but also it has no ability to store the memory. If writing new memories is a function of brain activity, then no one should remember NDEs at all—so all these physiological reasons are but moot points. Dissociative amnesia is a post-event psychological reason for being unable to access the memory, not something that affects the initial storing of the memory, so this could still stand as an explanation for the lack of memory.

The fact that memories cannot be made and stored in the brain during an NDE raises questions about where the memories are indeed stored. See the appendix if you are curious about this.

2. WHY MIGHT THE CONSCIOUSNESS NOT DETACH FROM THE BRAIN?

The second possible explanation for the low incidence of NDEs—namely, the 80 to 90% of CAs that do not result in one—is somewhat supported by the data from studies mentioned earlier, where some patients who had more than one CA experienced only one NDE. Of course, it could be that, because of different procedures or circumstances involved in each of the CAs, their memory was affected to different degrees, but it could also be other reasons that are not obvious.

Again, referring to the idea of spiritual aptitude, it may be that people who are more spiritual due to genetics have a greater natural ability to "disconnect" their consciousness from their brains. If this ability is not an on/off ability, but rather exists as a spectrum, like most abilities, then it makes sense that some patients who have more than one CA on two different occasions, will have only one NDE.

To explain this, imagine someone who is a professional golfer of modest ability. On occasional days he may exceed his normal ability and win a tournament, but on most he will be placed in the middle of the field; whereas a golfer of high ability should consistently lead the field. For similar reasons it is possible to imagine that someone who is very "spiritual" will always have an NDE (or always remember it), whereas someone who is spiritually less sensitive may experience or remember an NDE only on rare occasions.

Which leads to another possible reason: the individual may be in a state between having an eternal soul and having a material-bound, dying soul. The eternal light of the soul may be flickering due to the lack of spiritual exercise or practice, but there may still be hope.

While this is all highly speculative, and somewhat imaginative, nonetheless it is a possible explanation given the evidence.

Another explanation sometimes offered is the idea that NDEs happen only when there is a benefit from the learning the person will gain. Perhaps the older you get, the less likely you are to benefit from an NDE (the difference in NDE rate due to age is discussed in the next section). You are a "leopard whose spots cannot be changed," even by something so profound as an NDE. Your eternal destiny will not be altered by an NDE.

3. 80–90% OF ELDERLY HUMAN BEINGS' CONSCIOUSNESS IS INCAPABLE OF PROGRESSING TO THE NEXT DIMENSION

There is a third potential explanation for why only 10–20% of people who have a CA report an NDE. Namely, at the time of their CA, their consciousness—from an eternal perspective—is dead or dying. It has become so entwined, so enamored with the physical dimension in the world surrounding us, that it is unable to escape this material dimension—or stronghold—it inhabits and eventually dies with it. It has been "materialized."

Another thought is that some people are born with only this type of material soul, which leads to the question "Is it possible for some people to be born without an eternal soul?"

No. While I personally believe that most animals have a different level of consciousness to humans, I do not believe that having a fully functioning and potentially eternal soul is an accident of birth. All humans are born with the capacity to escape the physical dimension on dying and reach the "realms" or dimensions described and reported by countless NDErs—many of whom also had veridical OBEs.

This position is strongly supported by the unique evidence from childhood NDE reports. In general, there are fewer records of NDEs in children than in adults primarily because thankfully children are much less likely than adults to have a CA and be resuscitated. However, children do experience NDEs in ways very similar to adult NDEs. These children report an incredibly loving Being of Light, tunnels, heavenly dimensions, OBEs, and so on, but with one major exception: preteen children rarely report experiencing a life review. However, what is of particular relevance is the statistic that children who do have a CA and achieve ROSC are much more likely than adults to have an NDE. According to the book *Closer to the Light* by Dr. Melvyn Morse, which focuses on childhood NDEs from his years in pediatric medicine, about 80-90% of children who die and are resuscitated can recall some sort of NDE in contrast to only 10% of elderly adults, and this is supported by even more recent research.[17]

Why could this be?

There is little in the literature to suggest that children are less likely to suffer neuronal injury as a result of CA and subsequent ROSC, nor is there a radical difference in the medications used post-CA except perhaps for dosing, but this will be related to smaller body size and usually results in similar concentrations in the blood or central nervous system. Genetically, there is no difference between children and adults. Other than the enhanced learning abilities of children, and that adults have a slight decline in memory function with age (up to 25% in healthy seniors), the child's brain has no additional powers or functions that explain a 70- 80% difference in reports of NDEs.

Studies show that by age 70, the amount of information recalled 30 minutes after hearing a story once is about 75% of the amount remembered by an 18-year-old.[18] However, according to Alexandra Trelle, older people do remember the event occurring:[19]

Age-related changes in episodic memory are not "all-or-none" such that older adults simply cannot remember past experiences or recall fewer experiences than younger adults. Instead, aging is thought to affect the quality of one's memory, reducing the ability to recollect rich and detailed accounts of past experiences but leaving memory for more general aspects, or "the gist" of previous events relatively intact.[20] In particular, older adults tend to exhibit a decline in the ability to recover specific event details but display relatively intact memory for more general aspects of previous events.[21],[22]

The results from a meta-analysis of studies looking at changes in episodic memory with age (specifically recollection and familiarity) showed a mean decline in recollection of 34% between young (age <30) and old (age >60), and a mean decline of 14% in familiarity.[23] Recollection is the ability to remember details or specifics of an event, and familiarity is the ability to remember that an event happened. Neither of these numbers is close to 80% and therefore cannot account for the huge disparity in incidence of NDE reports between the very young and the old.

An interesting piece of research that looks at dream recall frequency showed similar declines over age,[24] with young adults recalling about ten dreams per month and the elderly seven dreams per month. There was a marked difference between males and females of all ages, with men having lower dream recall frequency than females, but still nothing like the difference observed between children and adults in NDE recall.

Another relevant piece of information is that the reduction in the number of reports of NDEs occurs gradually with age rather than as an immediate "cliff edge" at the age of 18. Dr. Morse saw 85% of NDEs in children, Ring noted 48% of NDEs in a mean age of CA of 37 years, Sabom saw 43% of NDEs in people with a mean age of 49 years, Van Lommel observed a rate of 12% having core experience with a mean age of 62 and in AWARE I, 9% had

NDEs with a mean age of 64. Thus, age and the frequency of the experience seem to be associated.[25]

Again, these differences are not consistent with changes in memory over age. Then, when you add the fact that a brain's memory-forming ability is of no relevance when the brain is not functioning, we need to abandon the idea that impaired memory function—whether it be age related, or due to injury to the brain from drugs or procedures, and so on—is behind this very significant discrepancy between elderly adults and children.

So, if there is no physiological explanation, why do most children have NDEs and most adults over 60 years of age do not? One possible answer is this idea of the materialization of the soul leading eventually to spiritual death when the host body dies. Maybe the longer we are exposed to the spiritually toxic material nature of the world around us and our desire to chase after and cling to the things of this world, the more "materialized" our soul becomes. Some, possibly even most, souls who live many years here, do not live beyond physical death.

Going back to a previous section, maybe they do survive physical death but are unable to recall the events because they were so appalling, as the process of the destruction of their world-obsessed souls is too traumatic to remember.

While physiological reasons for not remembering an NDE must ultimately be discounted because nothing "physiological" is working—including the ability of the brain to form and retain memories—it is still possible to include psychological reasons for not accessing or recalling memories. I quoted a Scripture verse earlier where Jesus warns us not to fear him who can kill the body. It was not the full quote, and I will leave that till the final chapters, where we discuss the findings from NDEs in light of the teachings of Jesus. For now, this last possibility of dissociative amnesia may well be related to the full quote.

All hypothetical, but also possible.

KEY LEARNINGS FROM NDES AND THE REPORTS OF NDERS

Below is a list of core "understandings" or "truths" that arise from NDEs and are common across all accounts where NDErs experience the different elements. This is the big picture that emerges despite any diversity and contradictions that appear in the details. It is what we will be using in the next section to measure the world's major religions:

- The consciousness can survive death.
- The consciousness is an independent entity, and while this consciousness may be very closely connected to everything else in a form of oneness, the sense of self, or of being a unique individual, is retained.
- There are spiritual realms that contain other spiritual beings. Some describe the realm of light as being heaven, and beings they meet there include dead relatives, angels, and a supreme creative Being of Light whom they often believe to be the source, or creator, or God.
- All who experience a heaven-type realm, and the "supreme Being of Light" report that our number one priority in life is to love, to treat each other with compassion and not to focus on the material. We are also here to learn and grow spiritually.
- Some people experience a hellish realm.
- There is a life review that does not feel judgmental.
- No one knows what lies beyond the boundary.
- They all come back, so no one has experienced true death.
- Most children who have a CA and achieve ROSC report NDEs, whereas most elderly adults do not.

CHAPTER 7: WHICH RELIGION IS MOST CLOSELY ALIGNED TO WHAT NDES TELL US?

At the moment, while people like me claim that NDEs are proven beyond reasonable doubt, the wider establishment does not accept this to be true. If you have read this far, or read my previous book, then I hope you share my view that we already have enough evidence to prove that NDEs are real. However, if you are of this view, you are currently in a minority. The vast majority of people either do not have a view, do not believe NDEs to be true, or are unconvinced either way.

If that state of affairs were to persist indefinitely, then NDEs and the implications they have would remain a somewhat niche subject. However, if there were a scientifically verified OBE, that situation would change overnight and interest would explode. I believe that day will come, but even if it does not, I believe understanding the relevance NDEs have to religion and vice versa is vitally important for all who understand the significance of these encounters with death.

Given that NDEs are the only empirical evidence we have for what lies on the other side, it is worth going through the exercise of determining whether any religions match this evidence. At the moment, the narrative is somewhat dominated by those who believe historical religions are irrelevant. In a recent interview, Dr. Sam Parnia was asked what NDEs tell us about religion. His response was as follows:

> As regards religion and even philosophy—of course, this is complex. Clearly throughout time and in every civilization, there have been some individuals who have proclaimed that our lives, actions, thoughts, and even intentions towards others are not meaningless and that we are not annihilated with death. Now for the first time in history, science is exploring death itself and what happens after death. What these experiences do provide is support for that line of thought. However, they do not support much of what else is associated with religion. For instance, people do not experience what their religions had taught them, and atheists and agnostics also experience the same review of their lives and lucidity with death. So, in short, this experience and what science is discovering at the time of death seems to transcend any specific religious doctrine. These experiences also do not support much of the rest of what is associated with religion—i.e., specific rituals, sociocultural aspects, and so on.[26]

Is he right?

RELIGIONS

There are many religions. As far as we know, and as Parnia suggests, humans have always had people in their midst who recognize the existence of a world beyond ours where consciousness persists. Moreover, it seems that many cultures have evolved with belief in a divine Being or beings who created our universe.

I grew up in a land with Christian traditions and believed in God from an early age. In my mid-teens, I looked outside traditional thinking and was open to the idea that all religions were the same. However, as mentioned earlier, toward the end of my teen years I had experiences that led me to believe that following Jesus was the best path.

Later, as my interest in NDEs and the reports we now have from the "other dimensions" began to peak, I was challenged to reassess whether my Christian faith was rationally tenable, or whether the more ecumenical position I held in my early teens better reflected reality. This ecumenical, supra-religious understanding is widely held and propagated by many in the NDE community, as evidenced in the quote above. They believe the empirical evidence of people's encounters with death do away with all religions. NDEs and the reports from the other side provide a new way. After reviewing thousands of NDEs as part of his research, Parnia said the following in *Lucid Dying*:

> In all these testimonies that we have studied, many were from people who followed a religion. Yet none came back to say that "in my review I learned how important it had been that I was following all the rituals of my religion." Everything simply boiled down to what they had done and the intentions behind them.

We need to take these assertions seriously and determine whether this challenge is credible. I am not interested in blindly following or proclaiming something that is patently false, which is one of the reasons why as a PhD organic chemist I dug deeply into the science of the origins of life. If I had found evidence that the first form of life could have appeared by natural processes, then it would have shown that my belief that God created life was questionable. That line of inquiry, detailed in my book *DNA: The Elephant in the Lab*, gave me an absolute conviction that I was on the right path and that the belief that life appeared as a result of a natural process is not only irrational, but scientifically farcical. The evidence shows that it was impossible for life to appear through natural means—no matter how old or vast the universe is—and that the very first DNA-replicating cell required intelligent input. My conclusion was that origins-of-life research showed extremely strong evidence in a creator God.

Just as I wanted to be certain that the foundations of my ruling philosophy based on a belief in the existence of God was correct, in light of NDE output I also wanted to make sure that the manner in which I pursued knowledge of and relationship with this God was correct. I asked myself, *Am I right to follow Jesus? Is there a better option? Are other options equally good?*

In my heart, I thought the perfect teachings and example of Jesus, combined with my amazing experiences as a follower of His should be all the evidence I needed, but my mind desired a rational response to these challenges. As I stated previously, for a long time I experienced some cognitive dissonance on this issue. That has disappeared and I have a clear view of the issues now. I have already begun to show a little of the path of reason that has led me to this clarity. In the remaining chapters I will lay that out fully. But it requires following a route that may seem upside down to Christians who never for a second question certain aspects of their faith.

NDEs potentially provide us with unique insight into the dimensions referred to by the different prophets. NDEs are eyewitness evidence that consists of glimpses of the afterlife that may inform us about what happens to our consciousness once our physical being dies. The core understandings of NDEs outlined at the end of the previous chapter capture the essence of the numerous reports that have been made. It is therefore possible to make a rational evaluation of whether any, all, or none of the spiritual leaders and the religions that formed around their teachings correlate with these accounts.

If you are a hard-boiled relativist, I must warn you to read no further. It becomes very clear that if you use the core truths as a yardstick then only one "prophet" stands the test fully, and therefore all others are inferior.

It is unfashionable to use the word "inferior" when describing people's opposing views, and many would regard it arrogant or offensive to use this word in the context of other people's religious belief. This is regarded in our modern world as a very personal issue and therefore sacrosanct. Many Christians also subscribe to this viewpoint and have consciously or unconsciously embraced religious relativism, which maintains that one religion can be true for one person or culture but not for another. No religion, therefore, is universally or exclusively true—religious beliefs are simply an accident of birth. That is very much the conclusion Parnia and others come to. Again, from *Lucid Dying*:

> It is also equally important to highlight that after they return, people do interpret and filter what they had experienced through their own personal belief systems, referring to the luminous, loving, guiding entity as Jesus, God, Mohammed, Krishna, angels, and so on. But as we studied so many diverse experiences, we came to realize these people were all talking about the same thing. A guiding being that is luminous, loving, and with enormous magnitude. The labels they used were attached afterward, but the essence of what was being experienced was the same, irrespective of what they called it.

Whether Christians like it or not, it is simply a fact that most people come back with their particular religious understanding enforced, and are therefore *allowed* to return with the understanding that their own religious figure is this Being of Light.

Does this mean that relativism is correct? Personally, I am of the view that relativism in all its different forms—religious or otherwise—is cancerous to reasoned thinking. Absolute truth on key matters exists.

While there may be different ways of describing something, there are objective truths, or facts, about that "something" that transcends subjective observation and description. This applies to religion just as much as it does to science. God either exists or He does not. God is either a he, she, it, they, or a multidimensional combination of them all that is beyond our understanding or ability to describe. This thinking may sound like relativism, but it is not. God is a specific something, even if he defies our ability to define that something.

There are clear, absolute answers to a number of questions in this regard that show religious relativism as nonsense and allow us to make objective assessments of whether a religion is inferior, equal, or superior to others with regard to its objective accuracy. If all the key religions and their prophets answer these questions equally well and in a very similar fashion, then it may indeed be possible that Krishna, Muhammad, Jesus, Buddha, and so on, are all equal. However, they do not. Let us see why.

Some of the key questions a religion needs to address are as follows:

1. Is there a God?
2. If there is a God, who is this Being? What is this Being like and how important is this being?
3. If there is a God, how does he tell us to behave?
4. Do humans have a soul capable of surviving death, possibly for eternity? If so, is it indestructible?
5. Is there a heaven? If so, what is it like? Who gets to go?
6. Is there a hell? If so, what is it like? Who ends up there?
7. Is there judgment at death?
8. Is there reincarnation? If so, what form does it take?

Prior to the era in which CPR provided us with thousands of NDEs, all we had to go on—with regard to deciding which religion best answered these questions—were our own subjective preferences and the arguments of various scholars and apologists from each religion. However, the central understandings from NDEs that rise above any noise of inconsistency on details, give us potential answers to some of these questions.

Is there a God? Yes.

Who is this Being? There are fundamental objective truths about the nature of the supreme Being of Light encountered in NDEs, who, for the purposes of this section we will call God.

NDErs report God as a unique and specific entity emanating light; as one of an indescribable and infinite love; one of complete knowledge; as powerful; as patient; as compassionate; as forgiving. While the subjective human-given name of this Being is disputed, the specific nature and characteristics are objective facts. These descriptions of God's character are specific qualities provided by ordinary living humans who claim to have met God in their NDEs.

We can measure these qualities against the prophets and teachings of each religion and therefore make a judgment about whether all religions equally reflect the characteristics and values of this being, whether some are better than others, or whether all are completely wide of the mark. This is what I mean by inferior or superior. Just as modern GPS is superior to a map drawn in the Middle Ages for the purpose of navigation, so some religions may provide a better understanding of who God is and how to access his infinite love. However, while a map drawn in the Middle Ages may be a thing of beauty and worthy of value, it may not help you get from A to B as well as GPS will! Equally, some religions may be beautiful and reveal some of the truth, but they do not quite get the whole truth. If you could choose only one and your primary need was getting from A to B, which would you rather have—a beautiful ancient map or the latest GPS (or phone)? I know a relativist would say the journey may be more fun if you get lost using the old map, but the fun ends if getting lost costs you your soul.

How does "God" tell us how to behave? We now have reports from NDEs that tell us what this Being wants. Again, no matter what the cultural interpretation of who this Being is, we are commanded first and foremost to be beings of love and to be compassionate. This is the central command and, again, is a truth consistent across all accounts from NDErs who have met the Being of Light.

This is where perhaps there is significant alignment across religions. There are instructions on avoiding an attachment to material things and treating all life with respect, and so on, that also align with the teachings of all major religions. If people stick to these commands, then their behavior is compatible with the desires of how our creator, the Being of Light tells us to live.

If the latter is true and is all that is needed, then it may be fair to say that all religions are equal. But what if each religion says other things that contradict the central teachings I have mentioned and therefore cause confusion? Or what if one religion provides better details and practices on how to attain this perfect way of living than another? What mechanisms do these religions provide to help us deal with failing? Which of these mechanisms seems aligned with what we learn from NDEs? These are issues that would clearly differentiate the different religions and allow one to ascribe inferiority and superiority in terms of whether they best represent the Being of Light.

Do humans have an eternal soul? If so, *is it indestructible*? Yes, to the first part, and possibly no to the second.

Is there a heaven? Again, if we take NDE understandings as empirical evidence pointing to the truth, then yes, and it is a place of unimaginable beauty. We quite literally cannot imagine how amazing it is. That is what people who have been there say. Then there are questions about whether we are still married in heaven—if we were ever married in this life—and other details. If a religious leader was able to provide correct answers on this kind of detail, then it is highly likely that he has unique knowledge of heaven.

On the subject of who gets to go, the answer is less straightforward. Many describe it as home—the place they have always belonged—which may imply that all souls are destined to end up in heaven. However, as discussed in previous sections, it is possible that some people's consciousness does not survive death. This is a point mentioned by some religions, but the answer of who this happens to is not consistently answered by NDEs. The picture is somewhat unclear. As I have said, many in the NDE community interpret this to mean that everyone gets to heaven in the end. That, however, is not a core understanding that rises above the noise of diverse accounts and therefore is not something we can use as a yardstick for the religions.

Is there a hell? Again, according to some NDErs, yes. I covered that in the section prior to this. So, the next things to consider are, which prophets talk about hell and how do they describe it? Anyone who knows would most likely be on the right track. NDEs do not necessarily shed light on specifically who ends up in hell, any more than they help us understand who gets to heaven. There are a number of accounts of atheists, including Howard Storm, who experienced hell before they were able to escape. Storm claimed that the reason he ended up in hell was very much related to his lack of belief in God and the impact that had on how he behaved toward others. He promoted disbelief in God, and attributed this as one of the reasons he ended up in hell. How he escaped is important to consider, and I will come to that in the final section. However, there are also accounts of Christians who ended up in hell.

Is there judgment at death? The answer to this is unclear. NDErs report a life review that feels more like a nonjudgmental review than a negative judgment. Regardless of whether this is judgment or not, it is clear that everyone will be required to understand their lives in the perspective of codes of conduct based on the core command to love others. I will go into the judgment aspect of this later, but it is missing from NDEs.

Is there reincarnation? On the occasions it is mentioned in verified NDEs, there is no suggestion that we take different forms of life, or come back with a different status. The context in which it is frequently mentioned is that of returning to earth because of a need to learn more.

So, these are the answers provided by the sum of NDE accounts to these fundamental questions. Given that we have answers from NDEs, can we all but dispense with religion, as Parnia seems to suggest? After all, we appear to have significant knowledge of God, heaven, hell, and how to behave. In Lucid Dying he says the following:

> They realize that the idea that "belief" in a religious entity alone is sufficient is wrong. What actually matters at the core of belief is how it directs your actions. Does it lead to selfless humanity, and the ability to put others ahead of yourself—be it your child, your friends, your patients, or simply strangers on the street—and does it drive you to gain greater knowledge?

There is some truth in this, and anyone familiar with the Gospels will understand that belief without response in the form of actions is not true belief, a subject I will return to later. But Parnia and other proponents of "NDEism" for a better word, seem to suggest that the religion, the following of a specific set of teachings, is secondary to the universally desired outcome of being a "good person." The knowledge we are given about a good person is that they will be "loving and compassionate." This knowledge is useful but, in my experience, on its own is insufficient to help us walk through this life successfully from a spiritual point of view. To do that, we need power—more specifically, spiritual power—and I believe this can be attained only through connection with the source of that power, God, through following the specific teachings of someone who had exceptionally accurate revelations of how we connect to that Being, and spiritual techniques or practices that help us attain that connection. The latter is essentially what constitutes religion.

Religions are sets of beliefs, usually underpinned by sacred texts that are records of the teachings and behaviors of their founders, prophets, or gurus. They are then combined with "rituals" or practices that somehow enable this spiritual connection. These practices are often about how best to detach our consciousness from daily distractions and connect with a higher Being through meditation, reflection, prayer, or worship. Also, they provide examples of humans who give us a lead we can follow, someone who (ideally) displays the behaviors they teach. We humans need that example on which to model ourselves: "This is what he taught, and this is an example of how you put that teaching into practice." Without this example we either give up and say the way is impossible or distort the teachings to suit our own behaviors.

NDE accounts do not provide an example to follow or any instructions by which we can connect with our creator; therefore, "NDEism" alone does not have the potential to "transcend" religion. While the thousands of NDE accounts provide us with evidence of the potential outcomes of a life lived as God wills us to live, they fail to provide us with mechanisms or power to enable us to behave in this way. Moreover, while people who have NDEs have been overwhelmed by their experience and are more often than not transformed by it, people who have not had NDEs lack this evidential transformational experience to help them stay the course.

This was highlighted in the follow-up data to Van Lommel's Dutch study[7], where it was observed that those who experienced NDEs were highly likely to retain an interest in spiritual things, versus those who did not have this interest as they grew older. In fact, without an NDE it appeared that interest in spiritual matters declined as people grew older. An NDEr's experience provides a bridge between their minds and the eternal—it is like spiritual rocket fuel to break their attachment to this world. But just reading about NDEs, while momentarily uplifting, does little to help non-experiencers have that same long-term connection or lifelong power. Certain spiritual practices provided through "religion" enable the possibility of connection and provide evidential experience in this life. I can attest to that and will later.

Some would argue that New Ageism is the religion that emerges from NDEs. I understand that perspective to a point, but New Ageism is not a religion and is a term invented to describe a whole range of different, often occult, beliefs and practices. These subdivisions of the New Age phenomenon are actually in themselves distinct religions. Spiritualism is one of them, albeit this religion predates the term "New Age." It is quite popular among those who have an interest in NDEs and those who have experienced them.

Previous generations of my family were heavily involved in spiritualism, and I can say with experience that while it is true that there are other spiritual forces around us that we can access, not all are benevolent. Unfortunately, opening yourself to unknown beings beyond our understanding is not a good thing. Moreover, trying to decipher the direction of the New Age movement is like trying to understand the movement of a group of house cats or a box of frogs. I am of the view that suggesting people use NDE accounts as a basis of how to pursue spiritual enlightenment is no different.

Given this, I am strongly of the opinion that we need something better defined to help us connect with God and the power He makes available to us if we seek Him. We need the foundational understanding of who God is, the "rules" for living a godly or holy life, an example of how to live that life, and the spiritual practices that religion provides, but without the overt focus on these practices themselves as the goal. We need a religion that is not too religious! Does such a religion exist, and if so, how do we determine which one it is?

Well, although NDEs do not provide the route to spiritual awakening for non-experiencers, they do provide us with an objective set of parameters we can measure each religion against in terms of their ability to accurately answer the key questions above.

I am going to focus on the five major world religions, but this is by no means an exhaustive discussion. There are many comparative theology books out there that get into the weeds of this subject, but I do not feel it necessary to go into such detail. There are some core issues with two of the religions in terms of how they answer the questions I have asked, which immediately provide sufficient cause to relegate them.

I am writing this from a Christian perspective and primarily targeting my fellow Christians to provide them with armor they can use to defend themselves against what I believe will be a tidal wave of relativism—if Parnia's remarks are the standard to go by. Despite this Christian perspective, the arguments below are no less valid. Go ahead and cross-reference the answers from NDEs against each of these religions and their founders yourself to see if I am right or wrong. Having said that, all of these religions have some aspects aligned with learnings from NDEs. Also, I do believe that all those who truly seek God with all their heart, soul, and mind will find Him. Given this may be the case, why make it harder to find God than need be? One thing is for sure, religions are not the same and most definitely not equal in the context of this discussion.

HINDUISM

To say that Hinduism is a religion is not entirely correct. This is because it is more a collection of similar beliefs with common themes and practices that emerged over 3,500 years ago and is geographically defined as coming from India. In fact, Hindu Nationalism has become a hot political issue. That aside, Hinduism does state there is a creator God—Brahma—but they also have a number of other gods they worship. Depending on which Hindu sect you belong to, they may be regarded as being superior to Brahma. This is one of the key issues with Hinduism: it is not absolutely clear what it is, and therefore the idea that they believe in one God who is a distinct loving Being is not obvious.

Hindus believe in a soul and the reincarnation of this soul in a cycle of life and death, followed by eventual release from each cycle once you achieve a certain level of being. According to Hindu belief, everyone's soul comes from Brahma, and all souls will return to him. The ultimate form of enlightenment and achievement is to become one with this supreme spirit and return to an eternity of peace and rest. This state of rest may be somewhat aligned with what we learn from NDEs.

The way the different Hindu sects teach people to live is again somewhat aligned with what people learn from NDEs. It is about respect for all life. However, one topic that seems to strongly contradict learnings from NDEs is the diabolical caste system that classifies people's status according to their birth. It consigns hundreds of millions to poverty and "sub-human" status, while others are born at the very top of the pyramid.

With regard to heaven and hell, Hindus do believe in different "realms," ranging from good to bad. Some of these realms are a temporary state before reincarnation either as a human or another form of life. There are bad places and good places, with a final upper heaven for those who reach a sufficiently good level and do not need to be reincarnated. The places of suffering sound quite similar to some of the hellish or negative NDEs.

In general, it would seem that while it is hard to define what Hinduism is precisely, there are many aspects that suggest that the various teachers, visionaries, or initiators of Hindu traditions, at the very least, caught glimpses of the loving divine being, of heaven and hell and how to behave. It is quite possible that these early initiators had NDE-like or transcendental experiences and that Hindu traditions were born out of the revelations they shared. Ultimately, from my limited understanding, "good" Hindus are likely to behave in the way not too far removed from that of the Being of Light.

My ultimate assessment of Hinduism is that if you are able to ignore the abhorrent caste system and the fact that it results in horrific injustice, if you ignore the worship of "false Gods" (spiritual entities that are not the creator God), and do not pay too much regard to reincarnation as insects, then it has positive aspects to it. In the absence of other teachings, it would be passable as a religion that partially reflected the core truths revealed from NDEs. But there is competition.

BUDDHISM

Buddhism has its roots in Hinduism and was founded around 500 BC by Siddhartha Gautama, the original Buddha, or enlightened one. On observing that all life was suffering, he left his wife and child to go and find himself and the route to nirvana, which is ultimately the end of earthly or material thinking. Nice.

Buddhism is very popular among some Westerners for one reason: it is essentially an atheist belief. In Buddhism there is no creator God; nor is there an individual soul. I think I shall stop there because, despite the many good practices encouraged by Buddha, to be so widely off the mark when it comes to central elements of what we learn from NDEs, and indeed science, which clearly point to a unique creator God and unique individual souls, means it is somewhat irrelevant as a religion.

I suspect that if everyone practised Buddhism, the world would be more peaceful and compassionate, but would not lead one closer to engaging with God. This is because Buddhism encourages the practice of meditation, but not a form of meditation focused on God or his teachings. My experience is that meditation is truly beneficial, and I reach a state of heightened awareness of everything around me and my place within that. I am able to observe my mind as a distracting voice and have discovered that "the real me" is not a product of my chattering mind but something beautiful and peaceful. I feel connected with everything around me and enjoy freedom and a sense of enlightenment. However, while I believe meditation can be useful if practised in a neutral context, I have experienced something superior to this, which I will discuss when I talk about Christianity.

ISLAM

Islam is the youngest of the world's significant religions and has existed for only 1,400 years. Its founder, Muhammad, is very well known, and his sayings and actions were recorded in great detail by his devoted followers.

Islam identifies only one God, who is reportedly merciful and all-powerful. There is a heaven and a hell, with judgment based on how good you are. Heaven is described as a paradise of gardens, which is certainly very much what we hear from NDEs.

I've spent a considerable amount of time in various Muslim countries and talked to many Muslims and ex-Muslims. Most of these people were wonderfully hospitable and respectful (to me anyway, but not so much to my female companion). Many millions of Muslim people live according to the values we hear about in NDEs. There are many good commands in the Quran, the Sunnah, and the Hadiths (the accounts of the life and sayings of Muhammad), and if these were all that was said on how a Muslim should live, then it would be fair to say that embracing Islam might be aligned with much of what we are led to believe the Being of Light wants from us. But it is not.

Some of the Muslims I met were very pleasant and respectful of others in most ways but had a raging hatred of Jews—to the point that I actually heard more than one say how much they admired Hitler! I was in my early twenties and fairly ignorant of Islam when I came across this dark anti-Semitism for the first time. I was not sure if this attitude was a result of their personal prejudice or due to the teachings of their religion, so I did some reading up.

The more I learned, the more I realized that not only is the Quran littered with texts showing hatred for Jews, but Muhammad himself was responsible for the deaths of thousands of Jews, Christians, and other unbelievers—

or "infidels" as they are called by Muslims—in his lifetime. His teachings and example have also resulted in the slaughter of many millions of people since his death. There are other acts supposedly committed by the founder of Islam recorded by his own devoted followers in the Hadiths that I will not print here because they are unspeakable, but it is clear where ISIS got their inspiration from. The fighters of ISIS and other warrior Muslims such as Hamas, Boko Haram, Hezbollah, and Al Qaida, to name but a few, base their way of living directly on the example of Muhammad, who in the later years of his life, became a successful military leader through his efforts to spread his new religion.

Islamic apologists will often cite peaceful texts for every violent text or example. However, one of the key principles in deciphering the Quran and other Islamic texts and determining which is the "correct" one is the principle of abrogation. In Islam this means the most recent edict by Muhammad on a specific topic is the one Muslims should follow. As much of the Islamic incitement to violence towards and subjugation of unbelieving men and women comes chronologically after the peaceful "Let's all live together" stuff, Muslims who support violent suppression of infidels are theologically correct. Moreover, the violence is not just limited to the battlefield, as Muhammad and his followers used sexual violence against unbelieving women, and girls.

Given this, large chunks of Islam and the latter part of Muhammad's life and example seem the very opposite of what we learn from NDEs about the way we are supposed to live. Muslim theologians would probably say that is all fine since they would argue that the Being of Light is none other than Satan. There are Christians who hold this view as well. Fine, let them believe that but, either way, I am of the view that Islam is not, on balance, a religion of love and light, and should be rejected by all those who wish to reflect the infinite unconditional love of the Being people encounter in their NDEs, and describe as God.

JUDAISM

Judaism is the religion of the Jewish people and is, for the most part, an ethnic religion—you are born into it or you can convert to it, but it is a bit of a process. It was founded by Abraham, who walked with and had very specific revelations from the one God about his being the father of a great nation. Various descendants continued in this relationship and eventually the people of Israel emerged, all following the one God, but with varying levels of success. Moses, many years later, had further revelations and was given the Ten Commandments directly by God, which formed the basis of how God tells humans to behave. The concept of heaven is mainly understood to be the home of God and perfect beings. There seems to be less clarity about the destiny of the human soul at the end of this life.

For the most part, the Old Testament is a collection of documents recording the history of the Jewish people, the laws God gave to them through Moses, and some writings by kings and prophets about God and his plans for the Jewish nation.

The Jewish faith points to some of the elements described in NDEs, and believes the Ten Commandments are perfect. If everyone followed them, they would be 100% aligned with what the Being of Light requires of us. Also, the Old Testament, taken as a whole, reads like a love story between a God of infinite patience and love and his troublesome ill-disciplined lover. It is a testimony to the character of God in the face of repeated human insults. As a Christian, I hold the Old Testament in very high regard. It prophesies the coming of Jesus—the Messiah—and provides insights into God's character through the numerous revelations He provides and His endless patience and love for the Jewish people.

There are aspects of the Old Testament that do not seem aligned with what the Being of Light wants from us, particularly the wars and violence between different tribes or races. Also, there is a lot of judgment and punishment for seemingly trivial infractions of laws that were added after the Ten Commandments. However, these issues are entirely addressed by Jesus, who while stating that the Jewish laws were God's will, nonetheless went on to "clarify" and simplify some of them as well as go on to hold us to a higher standard.

CHRISTIANITY

So far, all of the religions mentioned are "inspired" or "revealed" by human beings. As such, everything they have said is something we would have to trust as authentic. But humans are flawed and, in general, their ability to communicate directly with God is also flawed. So, it is quite possible that while these men had glimpses of truth, they were unable to grasp the whole truth. As a result, it is easy to argue that their religions were not full revelations of what the Being of Light, or God, wants from us.

However, there is one Human Being who made an extraordinary claim about Himself that was above all the others.

The Christian religion is based on the teachings and life of Jesus Christ, which are recorded in the four Gospels by witnesses—or those who spoke to witnesses—of extraordinary events that occurred just under 2,000 years ago.

Because Jesus was born a Jew, and declared that the laws of God written in the Torah by the Jews were to be upheld, and because He referred to prophecies about the Messiah as being prophecies about Himself, Christians include the Old Testament in their holy Scriptures. However, outside of the Ten Commandments, Christians do not apply all the other myriad rules and laws declared by Moses in their lives—Jesus' death on the cross exchanged the laws of Moses with the free gift of salvation through grace. Rather, they follow the updated and much simplified commands of Jesus, and the guidance given by the apostles in various letters and writings that came after the Gospels.

So how do Jesus' teachings measure up to the answers from NDEs?

Jesus said He is the "Son of God," which clearly aligns in terms of stating the existence of a God. In fact, he goes further than saying that he is the Son of God when you read between the lines, which I will do in the next chapter.

The essence of the teachings of Jesus are summed up in His command to love God with all your heart and love your neighbour as yourself (see Matthew 22:37–39). He goes even further and says we should also love our enemies (Matthew 5:43) and show compassion to everyone (Philippians 2:1–2). We must forgive others when they do us harm, even if they do so repeatedly (Matthew 18:21). We must not focus on material wealth (Matthew 6:21), but rather serve others and God, even to the point that we may need to put our lives on the line (Matthew 16:24-27). While we must be ready to die for what we believe in, there is no justification for non-defensive violence, and many would argue even for defensive violence. That, after all, was precisely how Jesus lived. He teaches us that we must trust in God and have faith in Him. Much of this is closely aligned with what we learn from NDEs.

His final command was for Christians to spread the good news that He had shared; namely, that sinners (meaning everyone) who believe in Jesus will be forgiven and will not die but have eternal life (John 3:16). This is a spiritual rebirth that allows those who believe in him the opportunity to completely wipe their slate clean and be reborn in this life.

Jesus describes God as a loving Father who will give us every chance to turn away from our life of earthly desires and be reconciled with Him. He wants everyone to share His eternal kingdom with Him. This is what we understand from the Being of Light: love, compassion, and acceptance lie at the heart of the descriptions NDErs give of God.

Jesus clearly states that humans have a soul when He says, "What profit is to a man if he gains the whole world yet forfeits his soul" (Matthew 16:26). This lays claim to the fact that the soul is destructible, which again may align with what we learn from NDEs.

Heaven. Jesus' descriptions of heaven are those of a paradise, of which He even provides details. For instance, when asked whether people are married in heaven, he says that marriage does not exist in heaven, but rather we will be like the angels (Matthew 22:30). His understanding of what heaven is like is so aligned with what NDE reports claim, it is as if He has actually been there. In fact, He states He is from there, which I will come to in the next chapter.

In terms of who gets to go to heaven, He says that those who believe in Him and obey Him will go to heaven. This is one of the crucial points on which some claim there is divergence from the teachings of Jesus and the reports of NDErs. A lot of people who did not believe in Jesus before claim to have experienced paradise in their NDEs, and some who claimed to have already believed in Jesus end up with negative NDEs, so on first glance this would appear to contradict what Jesus says. However, the specifics of who gets to go to heaven do not really emerge from NDE accounts due to the background noise of contradictions and divergence between accounts. Moreover, given there may be questions about whether the scenes NDErs experience are in fact God's heaven due to the existence of the boundary, we cannot take their claims about who gets to go as written in stone. We will look at this more closely later.

Hell. Jesus describes hell in various terms: a garbage dump, a pit, a place of burning, a place where the soul is destroyed, a place of isolation from the goodness that comes from God, and, most of all, a place of suffering where there is much "weeping and gnashing of teeth" (Matthew 13:42). Again, this is consistent with some of the reports from NDEs.

In terms of who ends up there, Jesus talks about those who reject Him and reject God. There is evidence of this from NDEs. Howard Storm says that in his NDE, where he went to hell first, he realized he was there partly because of his rejection and persecution of God and Jesus. Whether this happens to everyone who behaves like this, we do not know from NDEs. However, it seems that people who claimed they did not lead bad lives and were in fact Christian had hellish NDEs. Given this, it is apparent that NDEs are not clear on who ends up there. So, we cannot really measure what Jesus says against this.

Judgment. This is another issue where there may at first glance be a bit of deviation between reports from NDEs and the words of Jesus. Jesus describes judgment, not a review. You are assigned an eternal destiny—death in hell or life in heaven—based on this judgment. This contradicts the majority of reports of a nonjudgmental life review. Jesus does say there is nothing secret that will not be disclosed (Luke 8:17). This suggests first-hand knowledge of the fact that every single thing we have done, said, or thought will be reviewed by you and Him; otherwise, He is clear about there being judgment and division. Given that the life review was not final, as the NDErs came back, it is not possible to say whether judgment might have occurred had people stayed dead. Again, it is not possible to judge whether Jesus was aligned with NDE reports or not on this matter.

Reincarnation. Jesus does not say anything on this subject. He does talk about being born again, but that specifically refers to a spiritual awakening in this life as a result of receiving the revelation that Jesus was the Son of God and declaring Him as your spiritual King. The fact that He does not mention it means we cannot really make anything of His position on the subject. My position is, why take the chance? Make the right choice now. Make this life count in the eternal context.

Out of all the religions, the teachings of Jesus have best nailed the answers to the key questions when we are able to compare them with the answers derived from NDE "truths." Yes, there are a couple of points that need deeper exploration, which we come to in the next chapter. But I do not believe any of the key teachings of Jesus are at odds with our learnings from NDEs. In fact, they are so closely aligned that they point to His having first-hand knowledge of what is true. He says He is actually from heaven (see John 3:13). Moreover, not only did Jesus teach as though he had walked straight out of heaven—he lived that way. His life was unblemished by any wrongdoing, and filled with examples of self-sacrifice for others, including the greatest sacrifice of all, on the cross. He is the perfect model for us to follow, and entirely aligned with the kind of compassion described as desirable by those who have had NDEs.

The life and teachings of Jesus are best aligned with the core truths of NDEs; and the religion that comes a distant second, due to its lack of definition and clarity, in terms of alignment to the NDE truths is Hinduism.

So, if Jesus is head and shoulders above all the other prophets, let us look at NDEs from a different perspective. Let us see if the claims made by NDErs that I believe to be reported faithfully, match up to what Jesus states to be true, and where there is divergence or inconsistency try to understand why that might be.

I believe that performing this exercise reveals a little more about the nature of our existence than either NDEs or the Bible do alone. That is not to say that the conclusions one can draw are contrary to orthodox Scripture—in fact, they are fully aligned with some of Jesus' parables. However, they point toward a somewhat unsettling truth about this life on earth, our understanding of reality, and our place in the eternal scheme of things.

Are you ready to take the red pill? If not, put this book down now—you may never be the same again if you do not!

CHAPTER 8: UNDERSTANDING NDES IN THE LIGHT OF THE GOSPELS

Now we are going to get some answers. We are going to look at whether NDE heaven is God's heaven, whether the claims of universalists are true, whether the Being of Light is actually God, whether there is a final judgment. We will also investigate whether the soul is destructible, and if it is, who survives, what is reality and a little bit about what we are able to glean from NDEs and the Bible on the structure of and relationship between spiritual realms.

The way we will do this is by understanding NDEs from the perspective that because they lack consistency on many things other than on the "core truths," we must look at what Jesus says on each subject and use his teachings to draw conclusions as to the true nature of NDEs and what they really tell us about our existence. Not only do the words of Jesus clear any mist of confusion, but NDEs in turn provide us with more clarity about some of the things Jesus reveals to us in his parables.

Why should we take the words of Jesus as the final word?

Well, first, we just saw that out of all the "prophets" he was the one who had the most complete understanding both of the afterlife, as revealed by NDE core truths, and of God (if that is who the Being of Light is). Second, and of more consequence, Jesus made the astonishing claim that he is God.

Like many Christians I struggled with that one for years, often citing the Bible to point to the fact that Jesus himself places God as a higher authority. However, after much thought and prayer, the mist began to clear and I came to an understanding of the "Trinity" (the Father, Son, and Holy Spirit) that clarified everything. The words members of the Church of England sometimes use to describe the Trinity made it so much simpler—God the Father, God the Son, and God the Holy Spirit. They are all different persons forming the same being - God. There is only one God. God as the Father, God as the Son, God as the Holy Spirit.

Now, in our time-bound, finite, and material understanding of things, this concept seems impossible. But when you begin to understand the nature of the created "reality" around us, then things become much simpler to accept, even if we do not fully understand. As I said before, subatomic chemistry and quantum mechanics give us an understanding of our surroundings that points to their being somewhat illusory in nature.

It is entirely consistent with Christian teaching to understand the world around us as a created environment. However, because we feel like we are living in a material world, we understand this world only in material physical terms. But what if that is a lie we have unwittingly created for ourselves? What I mean is that the nature of what we see may not be what we understand it to be. To say that is not heretical, just as saying the earth goes around the sun is not heretical. Once upon a time, the latter was deemed heretical and Galileo Galilei was imprisoned for showing it as a fact, because the church had made assumptions about the solar system and our place in it that were incorrect. The same could be argued about our current understanding of the universe itself.

Before we take a few more steps down the rabbit hole, I want to point out that I am not trying to remove the mystery and wonder from our observation of creation and our existence. You could argue that much of that has already been done by scientists! Although, as a scientist I think the opposite. When you acquire the knowledge that allows understanding of things, your wonder only increases—even if the mystery evaporates. If mystery is just ignorance, then we are best to do away with mystery.

Our knowledge has increased. Our scientific knowledge through the scientific method and our collective human knowledge through experience have increased vastly, and with computers and the internet, exponentially. When it comes to explanations of existence, the recent knowledge from NDEs helps provide further understanding, although at the same time creating new mysteries. However, there are some things that once mysterious are now plain as day. Let us discuss those and their implications, especially when it comes to who Jesus was.

The universe is the result of God's imagination and his creative power, but our understanding of how it exists, what it is, is only from the perspective of being inside it. For God to come and walk among us while at the same time existing outside this created environment is entirely a possibility given it is his "show." I know I am tinkering with philosophical idealism here—the belief that we are living inside a mind or a simulation—but I am not saying that. However, I will come back to that in my final thoughts as I do believe it is a very important issue that needs addressing.

What I am saying at this stage is that we limit our expectations of what is possible by our limited, self-imposed, understanding of the environment in which we exist. Jesus, if He is God, as He claimed, does not suffer from those limitations.

So, what is the evidence that Jesus is God?

First, He said who He is:

The Pharisees and the teachers of the law began thinking to themselves, "Who is this fellow who speaks blasphemy? Who can forgive sins but God alone?"

Jesus knew what they were thinking and asked, "Why are you thinking these things in your hearts? Which is easier: to say, 'Your sins are forgiven,' or to say, 'Get up and walk'? But I want you to know that the Son of Man has authority on earth to forgive sins." So he said to the paralyzed man, "I tell you, get up, take your mat and go home." Immediately he stood up in front of them, took what he had been lying on and went home praising God. Everyone was amazed and gave praise to God. They were filled with awe and said, "We have seen remarkable things today." (Luke 5:21–26)

Now when I say that Jesus said He is God, he never actually came out and said those precise words, but inferred them in two ways: performing acts only God could—miracles—and saying things only God could say.

Only God can forgive sins; so, when He told people their sins were forgiven, He knew full well that He was doing what only God could do. On this occasion, to emphasize His point He showed something else only God could do effortlessly—perform an incredible miracle of healing.

Even today we regard miracles as miraculous, inexplicable, beyond the capability of man through natural means, as supernatural. However, if you consider that this entire environment in which we live is created, somewhat illusory in nature, and can be rearranged according to the will of someone who has the knowledge of how to rearrange it, the miracles become much less miraculous. That is not to downplay the significance of what Jesus did, but it is just to put into perspective what He did.

Jesus made the environment in which we live. To restore sight, to connect tissue, to calm a storm, to defy gravity, to change H2O (water) into EtOH (wine) was easy for Him. That is why He says that if you have faith it is possible for you to move a mountain. To Jesus a mountain is a quantum mechanical illusion, and if you have that understanding and the ability to manipulate the environment, then you can move it. Now Jesus knew that He had to draw the line somewhere. His walking on water had completely freaked out the poor disciples—imagine the response if He had suddenly moved a mountain! The whole world would have been forced to believe in Him. That, my friends, hints at the key to understanding all of this. But I will reserve the discussion on the requisite balance of knowledge to allow choice until we have completed our full assessment of the implications of NDEs in light of Jesus' teachings.

In the twenty-first century, man performs "miracles" every day. Talking face to face to someone on the opposite side of the planet on a wireless handheld device is ordinary to us now, but to people alive even a century ago this would have seemed like a miracle or magic. We have learned to manipulate our environment through our understanding of the laws of physics to perform what is an apparent miracle.

As an aside, this is why as a scientist I accept the fact that Jesus was born of a virgin. There are women today who have children who have never in their lives had sex with a man. We do not regard that as a miracle, and yet the most brilliant scientists alive today are like toddlers playing with their Lego compared to God when it comes to the ability to manipulate the environment. In fact, for me Jesus could not have come from human genetic stock. His "code" would have needed to have been so perfectly fine-tuned to receive the Spirit of God within his body that it would have needed to have been specially created, and not the result of random muddling of genes. The "virgin birth" makes complete sense when seen in that light.

Through His "miracles" Jesus showed that this world was His creation. He understood that to say in public that He is God was too much for most, but He nevertheless all but said it:

Then Jesus cried out, "Whoever believes in me does not believe in me only, but in the one who sent me. *The one who looks at me is seeing the one who sent me.* I have come into the world as a light, so that no one who believes in me should stay in darkness." (John 12:45–46; my italics)

Then in John 14 He says words we will revisit when discussing universalism:

Jesus answered, "I am the way and the truth and the life. No one comes to the Father except through me. If you really know me, you will know my Father as well. *From now on, you do know him and have seen him.*"

Philip said, "Lord, show us the Father and that will be enough for us."

Jesus answered: "Don't you know me, Philip, even after I have been among you such a long time? *Anyone who has seen me has seen the Father.* How can you say, 'Show us the Father'? Don't you believe that I am in the Father, and that the Father is in me? The words I say to you I do not speak on my own authority. Rather, it is the Father, living in me, who is doing his work. *Believe me when I say that I am in the Father and the Father is in me*; or at least believe on the evidence of the works themselves. (John 14:6–11; my italics)

Jesus said he and God were one and the same. His physical body may have been the "Son Of God" but his spirit was that of God Himself. He showed the disciples through "miracles" that He was God—the master of all creation. These men, after Jesus's death, were so utterly convinced by what they had seen with their own eyes that they went out across the world to spread the message they had been given facing relentless hostility and violence. Most, if not all, died gruesome deaths in the belief that this was preferable to staying silent and disobeying Jesus' call to spread the word. They believed beyond any doubt that they had been given the command from God, the creator of the universe. This certainty came from one final miracle that confirmed exactly who Jesus was and is related to the answer to the question I pose on the cover of this book. I will come to this at the end of this chapter.

For now, let us consider what the various subjective accounts from NDErs, and their inconsistencies, mean in the light of this understanding that Jesus is God:

IS NDE HEAVEN GOD'S HEAVEN?

Quick answer: "No one has ever gone into heaven except the one who came from heaven—the Son of Man" (John 3:13).

Long answer: Going by what Jesus says, no one has been to heaven except He who came from heaven. Does that mean that no one ever went to heaven other than Jesus before that? It is generally understood from the context of the exchange with Nicodemus immediately preceding these words that Jesus was saying no one alive has ever been to heaven, and only Jesus is qualified to speak of heavenly matters because he is the only one who actually came from there.

Given the ability to interpret this in different ways, though, I can understand why people may say that this preceded CPR-induced NDEs and therefore it is possible that people who say they have been to heaven, have been to God's heaven.

Personally, I am not convinced by this, and my intuition draws me back to the "boundary" beyond which NDErs tell us you cannot go if you wish to return to life on earth. I am also curious about what Paul meant by the "third heaven." No one really knows, even if they claim to. Was it a heaven outside of heaven in which God goes to meet visitors to the spiritual realm? Honestly, who knows? I think of my own experience in which I encountered

God. Can I say I was in heaven? It felt like it, but without ever having actually experienced heaven and that being confirmed, I would not know. At this point I am going to open a can of worms—the can of "spiritual realms."

What are spiritual realms? Well, to be honest we cannot know for sure, but we know of at least two: heaven and hell. Arguably, earth is a spiritual realm since it is inhabited by spirit beings—humankind, albeit squished into fleshly form. What if there are other spiritual realms or dimensions in which the spirits of people can exist, or experience the illusion of existing? What if any spirit can create the appearance of a realm? What if there is the possibility for an infinite array of these realms created by spiritual forces?

What if what if what if?

We just do not know, but here are the key reasons I do not believe the heaven reported in NDEs is God's heaven:

1. Because of what Jesus said about His being the only living human to come from there.
2. Because of the inconsistency and, in some instances, unreliability of reports. God's heaven would be consistent and how do we know which NDEs are fabricated?
3. Because of the boundary. Why would there be a boundary in heaven? It does not make sense.

In my view, and it is only that, I believe God's heaven lies beyond the boundary. Only there is full knowledge gained and a complete revelation of God attained. It is said in the Bible that no one can see the face of God and live. In NDEs people see a light, and may associate it with an identity, but I do not believe they see the face of God. Only in God's heaven do you see that.

Having said all of that, I do believe that some of these reports of NDEs are glimpses of what heaven is like and are a taster of what is to come on the other side of the boundary. Having discarded the weight of the body, people are able to experience this superior created place in a fulsome way and it is exceedingly good, but just like this world is a mere shadow of the NDE heaven, I suspect the NDE heaven is only a shadow of God's heaven.

What about the inhabitants of this NDE realm? The deceased relatives, the "spirit guides" or angels? Are they what they appear to be, or they are imposters, demons impersonating angels and dead relatives? This question extends to the Being of Light, but I will cover that in a segment of its own.

While I do not doubt the authenticity of many of the experiencers' reports, it is ultimately not possible to determine that what they claim to have experienced is what was actually going on. Given the inconsistencies and discrepancies between different accounts, I can understand why some Christians would reach straight for the demonic explanation, and they may well be right. My inclination is that something more subtle is going on, and here we go back to moving mountains.

Jesus revealed who He is to a relatively small group of people and performed His most incredible miracles, like walking on water, in their company only. He provided enough evidence for word to spread, and for those who have ears to hear and eyes to see to believe, but for those who don't, they could obviously doubt the reports and choose not to believe. However, had he actually moved a real mountain, something that had been a part of the landscape for millions of years and part of the conscious experience of everyone alive in that region at the time, then there would have been no room for doubt available, and people through reason would be forced to believe He is God. Jesus created a balance of knowledge that created a perfect tension between the positions of belief through faith and disbelief through doubt. This is God's plan for our lives: for us to choose him. If this tension created by the balance of knowledge does not exist, then we are not choosing Him—we are compelled to believe. I will come back to this again a number of times, but for now let us consider this heavenly realm, or realms, in that light.

If NDErs came back with exactly the same specific messages and descriptions, then their testimonies would be seen much more as fact than as a bit of a mess, albeit a mess with some defining truths. As such, in the event that OBEs were scientifically proven, as I believe they will be one day, then by inference the precise nature of this heavenly realm and its inhabitants would also be proven. Some in the NDE field like to make out that this is indeed the case. In fact, I myself went some way down that path in my previous book but, having become aware of the divergence of accounts and differences in descriptions, I can now see that this inference is not a correct conclusion to draw.

God may be allowing a redress in the balance of knowledge in favor of our understanding that life does not end with physical death, in many ways putting us back to where we were pre-Darwin. But, at the same time, there must still be questions that are answered only by really searching and at some point taking a leap of faith.

Is God allowing NDErs to be deceived by angels, or demons, and so on? Maybe.

"No!!" I hear you shout. "God would never allow that!"

Well, I have news for you. He already allows you to be deceived right here in this world in which we live. According to Jesus, whom we have established was most aligned with core NDE understandings, and was God according to his disciples who died declaring it, Satan is the lord of this world, and is also the Father of Lies.

We are placed here in this created place intentionally by God to find him in a testing environment.

Let us face it, we know of at least two occasions where Satan asks God if he can mess around with God's people: Job and Jesus' disciples. To be clear, Satan and God are not pals and are not equals. Satan is subject to God's authority, and is described as the enemy, but at the same time they do seem to be in dialogue about the testing of humans, and God has allowed Satan a lot of authority in this created world.

I know this may seem horrible for Christians to contemplate, but it is right there in the Bible, and if you do not believe that then just look around you! Every time you step outside the door you are tempted. You do not even need to go that far. We live in a whirlwind of spiritual suggestions and temptations that lead many to do diabolical things. Just open a newspaper. Let us be clear, though. Humans are culpable for the evil that occurs—they are the ones who chose to take up a suggestion to do evil. Without our willingness, Satan would be powerless.

As an aside, for those who use NDEs to suggest Satan does not exist because NDErs do not encounter him in hell, that is not surprising—because earth is his current home. As for Christians who do not believe in a real Satan as a specific being, read your Bible and look at what Jesus says about him. Jesus believed in Satan! In fact, they knew each other very well and for a very long time. Jesus, or God, saw him fall from heaven. Jesus says this; so, any Christian who denies the existence of the enemy of our souls is truly heretical and deeply deceived.

Back to NDEs. My totally subjective belief, using my bias about the reports of heavenly realms and heavenly beings, is that there are glimpses of truth, mixed with contradictory observations that may lead to a false understanding if pursued to a conclusion. Just like the world in which we live, and to which NDErs return, I believe this balance is intentional to allow humans choice.

Anyway, speaking of false understandings, let us move on:

IS UNIVERSALISM PROVEN TRUE BY NDES?

Short answer: "Enter through the narrow gate. For wide is the gate and broad is the road that leads to destruction, and many enter through it. But small is the gate and narrow the road that leads to life, and only a few find it" (Matthew 7:13–14).

Long answer: just as a reminder, universalism in this context is the belief promoted by many in the NDE community, and even some Christians, that everyone goes to heaven. However, Jesus' response to that is a resounding, "No, they do not!" It is a message repeated throughout His ministry. There is no doubt whatsoever that Jesus said most people will not experience eternal life. There is a lot to unpack in what He says on this subject, but first I want to address the widely held view within the NDE community, which they propagate to the curious and readily deceived public, that NDEs show everyone goes to heaven. This idea is nonsense. Even the evidence from NDEs contradicts this. I really wish I was wrong, but it is quite simply a fact.

First, it is widely documented that a significant number of people who have a CA and then achieve ROSC have a very negative, even hellish, experience. While Sam Parnia attempts to dismiss this as being related to CPR-induced consciousness, or ICU delirium, he is allowing his bias to ignore that the evidence is against this. Hellish NDEs are the same as heavenly NDEs except for the destination. So, right there the universalist stance is blown out of the water. Some NDErs clearly do not go to heaven. Universalism dies on that hill (or in that pit).

Second, as I showed earlier, age-related memory loss alone cannot account for the huge discrepancy between those who are elderly and achieve ROSC after a CA and those who are children. Something else is going on, and I alluded to two potential explanations.

The first explanation I gave was that the "materialization of the soul" during this life made it earthbound and unable to ascend to heaven when the person's body dies. So, what happens to that soul at physical death? Does it just die along with the body as atheists believe to be the case for everyone, or will it be "destroyed"? This relates to the second potential explanation I gave for why so few elderly people recall their NDEs—dissociative amnesia. Let us consider what Jesus says: "And do not fear those who kill the body but cannot kill the soul. Rather fear him who can destroy both soul and body in hell" (Matthew 10:28).

Is the reason these people cannot recall their memories because the experience was so utterly horrific that their brain will not allow them to recall the trauma? Or has the decision already been made and nothing will change their eternal destiny?

I really wish I did not have this bad news, but the data from NDEs seems to support Jesus's assertion that the majority of people's consciousness will be destroyed at the end of this life, and possibly in a fearful manner. The lights do not just go out, though—you suffer so much that your soul is starved of hope and light and maybe eventually dies among the howls and screams of countless others going through the same. That is what hell is like according to some of the reports of NDErs who claim they have been there. Some Christians interpret the Bible to say that the lost soul is constantly and continuously 'destroyed' i.e. for eternity.

Again, unlike some overzealous preachers, I take no delight in this at all and am acutely aware that while I may have reason to believe I am saved, I also know I am held to a higher standard, something I will come to shortly.

Howard Storm only recently divulged the full extent of the horrors he experienced in hell. He had kept the worst details to himself for years because it was too traumatic and shameful to share. He was raped by hundreds of beings until there seemed to be no substance to what he felt was his physical body. You wish you had not read that. I wish I had not heard it. There are others who have hinted at similar experiences and suffered with post-traumatic stress disorder when they returned. I wish I could pretend that everything will be all right, but that is not what Jesus said, and that is not what the evidence from NDEs says. It is my moral duty to speak the truth and to say it how it really is, not how I would prefer it to be. Too many Christians sugar coat Jesus' message, but the truth is that while he was the most loving and compassionate human to ever walk this earth, he spent a lot of his ministry warning of the dire consequences of not obeying God, precisely because of his love for us. You can rail against that truth as much as you like, but it will not change it. I did for years, leading to cognitive dissonance and dangerously muddled attitudes.

Thankfully Howard Storm's story ended well. In his experience, despite never having prayed in the earthly dimension, he called out to Jesus from Hell in his NDE and was rescued. He then became a Christian pastor after being a rabid atheist. Does this mean we may be able to escape hell after death if we end up there? Maybe, but why take the chance when you are told how to avoid it in the first place?

Back to John 14:6: "I am the way and the truth and the life. No one comes to the Father except through me." And, "He said to them, 'Go into all the world and preach the gospel to all creation. Whoever believes and is baptized will be saved, but whoever does not believe will be condemned'" (Mark 16:15–16). And, "Very truly I tell you, whoever hears my word and believes him who sent me has eternal life and will not be judged but has crossed over from death to life" (John 5:24). And, perhaps most famously, "God so loved the world that He gave His only begotten Son, that *whoever believes in Him* should not perish but have everlasting life" (John 3:16; my italics).

It is clear that believing in Jesus, that he was who said he was, is the basis for guaranteed eternal life. Some Christians miss some of the additional nuances in what Jesus says and, given his disposition for speaking in riddles, or parables, it is wise to consider what other meaning may exist in these verses and others. I believe many fail to do this.

Firstly, based on the above verses, many Christians believe they are saved purely by virtue of the fact they believe Jesus existed, was God, and call themselves Christians. It is most certainly true that the first step to eternal life is putting your faith in Jesus. But belief in Jesus is more than words—it is actions. His brother James was very clear on this and gave short shrift to those who had words without deeds (James 2:14-26). Some Christians will counter this by saying you are not saved by your works, as they are never enough. This is true: you are not saved by works alone, but you are not saved by words alone either. If you do not start acting differently, behaving differently, in other words repenting, then your belief is not real and your words are empty. If you believe in Jesus, then you believe his words, and they are full of teachings on how we should behave, and these teachings are based on two fundamental principles. One is related to one of the core truths from NDEs that we must love other people. The other I rarely, if ever hear, from NDE accounts:

> "Teacher, which is the greatest commandment in the Law?"
> Jesus replied: "Love the Lord your God with all your heart and with all your soul and with all your mind." This is the first and greatest commandment. And the second is like it: "Love your neighbour as yourself." All the Law and the Prophets hang on these two commandments. (Matthew 22:36–40)

The first and most important commandment is to love God with all our heart, mind, and soul. That seems to be missing from the to-do list NDErs come back with. What is even more astounding for me is that these people claim to have met God, that he is awesome, but do not make meeting him again their number one objective on returning. Having said that, I myself can hardly point the finger after not immediately following up on my own experience!

Many, as I did, find organized religion an obstacle to connecting with God, but if you seek, you will find. For instance, the church I attend, which on the outside—a small ancient Church of England church in a sleepy village in rural West Sussex—would seem like the last place you might have a radical encounter with God through his Holy Spirit. But twice every Sunday morning it is full to bursting with people who are connecting with their maker, who are deeply in love with God and Jesus. Sometimes the atmosphere is so thick with his presence that people are on their knees weeping with gratitude, or dancing in the aisles with joy. Worshipers travel from miles around to attend these incredible services. It will not be long before they need more services! I admit, in my experience such churches as Ashington, part of the Chanctonbury Parish, are not the norm, but there are others out there that come close. For me, when such encounters are so spiritually enriching, loving God is easy — obeying him, though, is a whole other kettle of fish!

That is where the second command comes in. Love your neighbour, everyone you encounter in life, as yourself. Jesus gives enormous detail on how to do this in his teachings. He also showed us through his daily sacrifice of himself and the final sacrifice of his life. This is in fact how people are taught to treat others when they are having their NDEs, and many come back transformed and live their lives for others. That is great, but if they do not prioritize connection with God, they will lack the fuel and knowledge of how to do it effectively.

So, Jesus said that believing in him will result in salvation. But what about those who do not believe? Are they all condemned to death or hell?

Many Christians believe that all who have not professed faith in Christ will perish. This led to the rather absurd belief among some Catholics that if a baby has not been baptized its soul will perish. Nonsense.

As another aside it is an extremely interesting and pertinent fact that children who have NDEs do not have a life review. It is the only element that differs from adult NDEs. My interpretation is that children are learning, they are not ready for any form of judgment. Jesus welcomed children and warned about leading them astray. I am certain that children go straight to heaven.

(I also believe that teachers who shove harmful ideologies down children's throats will experience a very different outcome—Jesus is clear on that too.)

To understand Jesus' position on whether not believing in him results in a lost eternity you need to read His words in full. I personally believe they are inclusive, as in if you believe fully you will be saved, but not entirely exclusive, in that not all who do not believe in him because they have not heard of him will perish. It has to be said that this is a moot point because these latter circumstances are extremely rare in today's world. Moreover, the discussion is hypothetical and only applies to people who are not involved in the discussion since those discussing the subject know about Jesus! It is a strawman used by atheists to distract attention away from their own predicament. However, let's cover it for completeness sake.

In Mark 16:15-16, Jesus tells his disciples to go and preach the message to the whole world, and those who believe will be saved and all those who do not believe will be condemned, but you could argue that they had to hear the message first to be condemned and that by not hearing the word they cannot be condemned. Who today has not heard of Jesus? However, even the position that those who have not heard won't be condemned, is dismissed by Paul when he talks about God's divine nature being clear to all since the beginning of creation in Romans 1:20. What about Jesus's position?

John 5:24, "Very truly I tell you, whoever hears my word and believes him who sent me has eternal life and *will not be judged*" (my italics). In other words, if you believe in God through Jesus, then live your life as he commanded, doing your best every day to follow him, and asking forgiveness daily for your failures, and trying not to repeat them, then you will "bypass" judgment. (I am aware that there are passages that refer to all Christians being judged, but because of their faith they do not experience the deserved condemnation. From here on when I refer to Christians "not being judged", understand that I mean the expression to refer to the consequences of judgement – condemnation). But how do the words from John 5:24 apply to those who have never encountered Jesus? Will they experience God's judgment and punishment? Christians, inspired by Paul in Romans 2:12, argue that because everyone sins, and God is perfect, everyone is condemned without faith in Jesus. Is this true? Possibly, but one also needs to consider the following words of Jesus: "If I had not come and spoken to them, *they would not be guilty of sin*; but now they have no excuse for their sin" (John 15:22; my italics).

Does this mean that those who have not heard the words of Jesus, or the Ten Commandments, are not guilty of sin because they did not know what sin was? Maybe, but the context of these words should be considered. Jesus was specifically referring to some of the Jews who hated him and his disciples and denied that he was from God despite seeing his miracles.

There is another verse, again one that is a double-edged sword, in which Jesus seems to make it clear that God shows his mercy to those who do not believe in Jesus because they never encountered him. Even if they did things deserving of punishment, their punishment would be less.

> The servant who knows the master's will and does not get ready or does not do what the master wants will be beaten with many blows. *But the one who does not know and does things deserving punishment will be beaten with few blows.* From everyone who has been given much, much will be demanded; and from the one who has been entrusted with much, much more will be asked. (Luke 12:47–48; my italics)

There are other clues as to what may happen to unbelievers who never encountered Jesus. In the Gospel of Matthew, Jesus' words "None can come to the Father except by me" are not used. That does not mean He did not say them, but maybe just that Matthew felt they were not the central focus of His teaching. John, the other Gospel writer who was a disciple, clearly felt these words were central, but even if you take John 14:6 to be the ultimate word on this, there is a bit of a twist. In one breath Jesus does indeed say that none can come to the father except by Him, but then in the next he says that He and the Father are one and the same (John 14:9-11). Now that creates a conundrum for Christian exceptionalists, because it would not be a totally unreasonable extrapolation to say that Jesus is implying that anyone who comes to God will be saved. If they encounter Jesus but reject Him, that is a different issue because he is God, but if someone has never encountered Jesus but truly seeks God, I am of the personal view they will find Him. Again, John 5:24: "Very truly I tell you, whoever hears my word and believes him who sent me has eternal life" (my italics). I honestly believe that those who truly seek God will find Him, and I believe that understanding is not inconsistent with the Gospels.

I am sure that some Christians will be getting hot under the collar at my personal position on this. Firstly, it is my position, although I am far from alone, and secondly as I said, it is only a hypothetical discussion that applies to such a tiny percentage of the earth's population that it is not really worth getting worked up about. Most have heard about Jesus, and either not bothered to find out more, or flat out rejected him. Jesus is clear what happens to them.

Let's see how starkly the teachings of Jesus contrast to NDEism. In *Lucid Dying* Parnia summarizes what people report from their NDEs regarding consequences of their behavior:

> Another facet of seeing the recalled experience of death through a religious lens is the realization that people didn't feel like they got away with their misdeeds. Nobody found that their misdeeds toward others were wiped off—forgiven away—simply because they believed in a particular religion or religious figure.

Most Christians would recoil at this, and I do believe, contrary to what he claims, that those who seek forgiveness for and truly repent of their sin here will not have to face the consequences after they die. This is the core message of the "good news" Jesus shares. However, I do believe that there is some truth in the above quote and it is worth repeating John 15:22: "If I had not come and spoken to them, they would not be guilty of sin; but now they have no excuse for their sin." And of course: "Not everyone who says to me, 'Lord, Lord,' will enter the kingdom of heaven, but only the one who does the will of my Father who is in heaven" (Matthew 7:21).

The teachings of Jesus are very clear about the responsibility and expectations placed on the shoulders of those who have had an encounter with Him, the living God. This is also where those who call themselves Christians, and yet do not believe with their actions, will indeed face judgement. Just believing with words is not enough (eek!). His warnings about those who fail to obey him are pretty dire, especially those who profess faith, but do not live in the way He commands. It seems terrible to believe in Jesus! But Jesus himself says, "My burden is easy and my yoke is light." Not because it is easy for us, but because through the power of His Holy Spirit, God's relentless love and grace, and his limitless capacity to forgive us when we genuinely seek forgiveness, if our hearts stay true to him, we will make it.

Let us bring this section to a close.

I believe the teachings of Jesus allow us to adopt a nuanced position towards unbelievers who never encountered Jesus, but not to believers, or those who reject Jesus. The way I see it, there are five groups of people, the first three being familiar from the parable of the sower:

1. Those who have had an encounter with Jesus, take His message to heart, repent, and do their best to follow His commands. They will fail, but they tried their hardest. They love God and rely on His love and mercy.
2. Those who have an encounter with Jesus, profess faith, but fail to enact his commands because they do not really try, or are distracted by other things, and are shallow in their belief.

3. Those who have an encounter with Jesus but reject Him.
4. Those who have never had an encounter with Jesus but try to find God, and even live the kind of life Jesus commanded us to.
5. Those who have never had an encounter and live sinful lives.

And the outcomes? Again, these are my thoughts. I believe they are consistent with the gospels, but I know others will disagree.

Group 1, straight to heaven. Now returning to Parnia's quote in which he suggests that those who believe in a religious figure still get to face the consequences of their wrongdoings. In this instance I believe he is wrong if those wrongdoings have been dealt with here on earth. What is the point in being told off and made to feel shame twice? I am deeply conscious of how rubbish I am at following Christ's example, and when I recognize I have done something wrong, I feel true remorse, bring it before God with shame, seek forgiveness, and try to repent, never to do it again. I do not always succeed, but if I do, like the amazing example of people in this category, really, what is the value in raking over the muck again? Jesus tells us we are not judged in this instance, and I believe Him. It is just and fair. Those who have believed in Jesus and lived a holy life will be entirely spared any judgment.

Group 2, may be on a sticky wicket. As alluded to above, I sometimes wonder if I am in this group. For people like me, it is time to take Jesus much more seriously. Heaven is by no means guaranteed just because we said the sinner's prayer—we need to live the sinner's prayer too! We need to repent, if we don't we face judgement (with condemnation).

Group 3 are in trouble. Jesus is very clear about this. If you reject Him, you reject God, and He says your eternal future is bleak. Do not kid yourself otherwise. You can change your mind, though.

Group 4 is the interesting one. God's Holy Spirit is everywhere in His creation. Some of those who have never had a real encounter with Jesus may still somehow be in tune with God's wishes for us. They seem to obey Him.

Notice in the passage from Luke 12 above, the one who has not been taught and does wrong will be beaten with few blows, what about those who do very little wrong? What about those who appear to do God's will despite never having had that personal encounter? Yes, they will be judged, but I would not be in a rush to condemn those to hell, as some Christians are. In many ways they put a lot of Christians to shame.

Group 5. God's Spirit is everywhere, and even if you have not had an encounter with Jesus, he whispers to your conscience. I believe they will be judged and perish, but maybe their "punishment" will not be so great, as Jesus teachings suggests. Maybe rather than being destroyed in Hell, they just die.

The miserable fact is, especially in Western society but really across the world now, most people are in Group 3, as most people on the planet will have at least heard about the existence of Jesus.

The West especially has turned its back on Jesus. They are in the biggest trouble. They had Him, but then threw him away. It is unbearable to watch it happen during my lifetime. Many Muslims reject Jesus as being God and instead choose to follow the teachings of a warlord. Jews missed the fact that their Messiah came. They rejected Jesus. Atheists everywhere, including Buddhists, deny Jesus. Hindus sort of accept Him, but do not allow Him the authority He should have due to their allegiance to multiple different deities.

The vast majority of humanity has now been exposed to Jesus at some point, and yet they reject Him. He warned us that would be the case, but it is so desperately sad. Billions, according to Jesus, face judgment with the certainty of a lost eternity.

Many use this to say that Jesus or God is nasty and spiteful. How can He condemn all these people to destruction?

They could not be more wrong. Even the most corrupt of people have some concept of justice and that actions or even inactions have consequences—wrongdoings deserve punishment.

God, in his wild love for us, gives us a way to avoid the consequences of wrongdoing. He invites everyone to His banquet in heaven through Jesus. He even allows His judgment to pass over the worst murderer if they believe in Jesus and repent. His grace and forgiveness for any sin are total for those who truly seek forgiveness and turn away from their past life of wrongdoing. So, all those who have heard about Jesus, and either rejected Him, or not bothered learning more when they were able, have effectively thrown away their RSVP to God's banquet in heaven. When their bodies die, where else is there left for them to go since the only place that sustains eternal life is in God's presence in heaven. Outside of that their souls will eventually perish. They may just die there and then, or they may go to a place filled with others of the same disposition, a place where there is no light and no goodness and according to NDErs filled with selfish, violent, abusive, hopeless beings full of rage, fear, and hatred. This is where they chose to be through the choices they made in this life, a place Jesus warned us all about if we did not seek forgiveness and repent.

GOD DID NOT SEND THEM TO THIS PIT OF DESPAIR—HE JUST DENIES ENTRY TO HIS KINGDOM BECAUSE THEY CHOSE TO IGNORE HIM

How is this not justice?

If you say to a teenage son on a Saturday night, "If you come home after 10:00 p.m. tonight, you will not get your allowance next weekend." Despite this, the son comes home at midnight. When the following Friday comes and his father withholds his allowance, he shouts at his father, "It's not fair!" What do you think of the teenager's protests?

Do not blame God—people choose their destiny for themselves. God came here and invited everyone, gave them a way home to the greatest feast in the most lavish palace in eternity, filled floor to ceiling with love, yet most had "better" things to do.

No wonder Jesus despaired!

So, there we have it. Not only is evidence from NDE research against universalism, but Jesus completely discounts this belief's naive and dangerous wishful thinking. He says the opposite; namely, that most will perish. He lays out a path, through Him, to guarantee your place in paradise. Because he so loved us he suffered enormous insult, persecution, pain, and a terrible death to enable it. It is not an easy path, but once you know it is there, you are in deep doodoo if you do not walk down it.

NDERS CLAIM THERE IS NO JUDGMENT. ARE THEY RIGHT?

Short answer: "I tell you, on the day of judgment people will give account for every careless word they speak, for by your words you will be justified, and by your words you will be condemned" (Matthew 12:36–37).

Long(er) answer: I am not going to belabor this, as a number of the quotes from the Gospels in the previous sections already mention judgment. Jesus is clear that He is the judge. John's Gospel suggests a negative judgment results in death, but Matthew's points to eternal punishment. Again, it is interesting that two men describing the same events use different terms, although some Christians interpret death as a state of eternal punishment. I have to admit I struggle with the idea that God would create a soul knowing that it could suffer eternal punishment. Death, I understand, but eternal suffering I do not; therefore, I tend to prefer John's wording and that it implies death as we understand it, but I may be wrong. Either way there is judgment for all who do not believe in Jesus.

So why do NDErs come back saying there is no judgment? Here are three things to consider:

1. While the life review does not always feel judgmental, in essence your actions are assessed or evaluated, so arguably this is a form of judgment. Moreover, there are those who report feeling judged. Many feel deeply ashamed of their behavior despite being accepted.
2. It is very, very important to note that the people who have NDEs have returned from clinical death. They did not experience irreversible death. It is possible that the life review happens in this context and is something the experiencer returns with and is supposed to learn from. How do they know there is not a different "final" judgment for those who do not return, which takes on a slightly different format with Jesus as the Judge? NDErs, despite protestations otherwise, are left in the dark due to this boundary, but the Bible is very clear that it occurs. In Matthew in particular Jesus talks about a specific day when all unbelievers will be judged. That day has obviously not happened yet.
3. How do we know they weren't judged in absentia? For all those who had the positive experience, maybe they were judged and allowed to continue to a heavenly realm (for now) without knowing it. Likewise, those who went to hell might actually have been judged but not known it, just like those doomed to destruction who never had any type of experience. Judgment might already have occurred.

In truth I find the issue of judgment in the Bible a little confusing, except for the consistent theme that true (active) believers in Jesus will not be judged (condemned). The specific timing and nature of the judgment etc is a matter of theological discussion beyond the scope of this text, but there is lots of detail for those interested.

IS THE BEING OF LIGHT ACTUALLY GOD?

Short Answer: "No one knows the Father except the Son and those to whom the Son chooses to reveal him" (Matthew 11:27) In other words, God in all his fullness as the God of heaven, God the Father, is only revealed to those whom Jesus chooses to reveal his full being.

It is really hard to tell if this being in NDEs is God. As I said before, the way people describe their encounter with this being echoes what I experienced in my encounter. I believe Jesus revealed the Father to me because my encounter was as a direct result of praying to Jesus. I never saw God, but I met Him. In the vast majority of these encounters in NDEs no one sees a being; they just see light, but know it is a being of infinite love, knowledge, and power. Some Christians say this is Satan masquerading as a being of light. I am not convinced—would Satan really be that good at impersonating God? Would he be capable of making a person feel so completely loved? Children report their encounters with this Being in the same terms as adults. I do not believe God would for a second allow children to be deceived in such a way.

My take on this, for what it is worth, is that just as NDErs get a glimpse of what heaven is like, they get a glimpse of God. He makes himself known to many people all across the world in this dimension, so why should He not in these experiences too?

Back to the words of Jesus. Is it not possible that for those who see this Being, Jesus has chosen to reveal the Father (and thereby Himself) to them? What they then make of that is their choice. If they do not respond by seeking this being out when back here, there may be negative consequences.

As for the cultural interpretation of who this being is, this is subjective. It is not possible for God to be Jesus, Krishna, Buddha, Muhammad, and so on. These persons were so utterly different, and while they at various points in their ministries shared teachings that were similar, the divergences in their other teachings and example are too stark for them all to be representing the same "source." No, only Jesus can be this being if you examine the evidence. Now, if someone does encounter a Being of Light that says it is Muhammad or Buddha, and so on, and it actually uses those words, rather than the person putting those words into its mouth, or just thinking it is them, then that would ring alarm bells about deceptive spirits. But in all the NDEs I have heard or watched, I have not encountered that yet.

In conclusion, I believe that the Being of Light may be God, but I am prepared to accept I am wrong on this.

I know God through my transcendental "dream" experience that happened only through my saying the Christian sinner's prayer, and therefore I must be true to the only conclusion I can logically draw from this—the path to God is through Jesus. My further amazing experiences of God reinforce this view because it is only through following Jesus and worshiping him with all my heart, mind, and soul, especially when among other devoted followers, that I get close to experiencing that intense love again. I will stand on that belief until the day of my death, even if it is the cause of my death.

JUST WHAT ON EARTH (AND OFF IT) IS GOING ON?

At this point we are coming near to the end of our journey to try to understand what NDEs are, what they tell us, how they relate to the teachings of Jesus, and vice versa. Before we come to a final very important point to consider, let us for a moment reflect on what all of this means. Seriously, what the heck is going on?

When you look at the information available to us from science, human experience, NDEs, religious teachings, and, specifically, the Bible, it is not unreasonable to understand the following to be true:

1. We live in a created dimension, the precise nature of which is hard to determine or define but, because we are in it, it feels real. However, when we are removed from it, we understand that it is not the true reality. Only when we are in our complete spiritual form will we be able to experience true reality. That is, our true selves. Aspects of the "illusory" nature of this earthly dimension are hinted at through our understanding of quantum mechanics.
2. There are at least two, or maybe even infinite, other realms or dimensions. The ones we know about from NDEs are a heaven-like place and a hell-like place. I have argued here that the heaven-like place is not God's heaven, so that may be another. But, given that each NDE experience seems different, it is possible that many more dimensions may be available. Much of this is speculative, but what is not speculative is that there are dimensions of greater "reality" beyond our own.
3. Our souls are able to survive death.
4. The choices we make during life in this created dimension determine the destiny and/or survival of our souls beyond the end of this extremely brief earthbound existence.
5. There is a God.
6. Jesus was God in human form.
7. God longs for us to be with him in heaven when our physical bodies die, and despite creating every opportunity for us to seek and find him, most do not make it and are judged unworthy to enter. While "the world" regards this as unfair, it is just, for God is just.
8. Believing, active, Christians are exempt from the consequences of judgment and will enter an eternal future in God's heaven when they leave this existence. Others may be judged and experience consequences according to their behavior. Those who did wrong will be "punished" according to their knowledge and understanding of what right and wrong is.

9. There is only one effective mechanism of dealing with past wrongdoings and guilt in this life: spiritual rebirth through active faith in Jesus Christ.

I wish to emphasize that while this created dimension in which we live may not be the final reality, given that every dimension is ultimately created by God, you could argue that nothing is in fact real. Down that road lies insanity!

My take on this is that while the dimensions we experience may be created or somewhat illusory, our existence within and response to events are not. "Reality" is our observations, actions, thoughts, experiences, and, most of all, our choices. Those things are real in all dimensions. The spirit or consciousness is the real phenomenon within these dimensions, and therefore the spiritual dimensions to which we are destined to go, if we survive the tests of this existence, are true reality. That may seem like philosophical idealism, and I will go into that in the final chapter.

I know some will be thinking that if God loves us so much, then He would make it easier, even obvious, to choose him. I will cover that in the final chapter as well, which follows this next section.

I do however believe we are given enough evidence to make an informed choice, if we seek that evidence. We do not need more evidence than we have. There may be readers who are still stuck on item 6 in the list above, "Jesus was God." This is a sticking point for many, but it is probably the most important truth to accept, even if it takes you a long time. There is one final piece of evidence regarding Jesus' being God that I now wish to discuss, and it answers the question on this book's cover.

DID JESUS DIE FOR NOTHING?

There are two key components of Jesus' death. The first is His sacrifice on our behalf; the second is His resurrection.

Now I do not fully understand the spiritual or scriptural mechanics of how the sacrifice Jesus made pays the "ransom" for our wrongdoings, but I accept that it does. It was important, even vital, that he suffered at the hands of men, that he endured the beatings, the insults, the execution when he had not done a single thing wrong, and that it was all in our place. I understand that it was a suffering that needed to be endured on behalf of the wrongs we have all done. The injustice of the pain He suffered was infinite because He had zero sins against His name, and that therefore the forgiveness of our debts is infinite if we believe in Him. That is the limit of my understanding. Those who choose to believe in Him, seek forgiveness, and repent are free from guilt in this life and the consequences of judgment after it. The price for the sins we have committed has been paid.

However, if Jesus had just died for this reason alone, even though it was the death of the only sinless human to ever have walked the earth, then His death would have appeared to many to have been for nothing. But He did not just die; He then conquered death: "God has raised this Jesus to life, and we are all witnesses of it" (Acts 3:23).

These are words from Peter's sermon to the remnant of believers on the day of Pentecost, at a time they were being hunted down by the Roman and Jewish authorities. Peter was a disciple of Jesus and had witnessed most of His ministry. He also claimed to have witnessed the risen Jesus. He believed so utterly in what he had seen that he would lay his own life down rather than deny what he knew to be true. All of the disciples, bar Judas, did the same, as did many others who had followed Jesus and witnessed the events of His life and resurrection.

Either these men were insane, or they knew that their claims were true, and that they feared lying about it more than a violent death. Why fear lying about this if a lie would spare your life? Because the resurrection of Jesus told them exactly who He was, and who He had subtly claimed he was all along. He was not just the Son of God, He was God the Son. He was God in human form. They were utterly convinced of this, to the point of death.

His resurrected body was the final and most compelling piece of evidence for His divinity He provided to his disciples. Not only did he rise from the dead with a body that had the wounds he sustained while being crucified, thereby showing death was conquered, but also his body was no longer a normal earthly body. It was of a form that was able to appear to people and then disappear, in different places all over the area where he had preached, and yet he ate food, and people could touch him. This body, which is beyond our understanding, finally ascended into heaven. It was a transcendental body, a body beyond this dimension, and final proof that Jesus was God. This is what those male and female witnesses believed to be true with all their hearts and minds. I believe their accounts, and many books have been written that show why everyone else should too.

If Jesus had just died, his death would have been for nothing; but because he was resurrected, he proved beyond any doubt to his followers that he was God, so his death and resurrection were the most important events in human history. They showed that God had walked among us, and therefore we should take note of what he said.

Therefore, we must measure NDEs in this light. Jesus' teachings and example are the ultimate authority, the final word on how to live. Now, as I said, because OBEs have been proven real, we must take many NDEs to be genuine accounts of what people experienced while they were outside of their bodies in these spiritual realms. Where there is absolute consistency of what is reported, then we must take that seriously and regard them as core understandings. When we do that, we learn that none of the core truths contradict Jesus' teachings, but where there are inconsistencies or contradictions, or where there are clues that point to a lack of completeness, we must default to the words of Jesus.

I hope I have done that faithfully so far in this book. As I said, NDEs reveal to us aspects of the spiritual realms that are mentioned in the Bible, but in greater detail. However, I believe NDEs do not answer some of the most fundamental questions; only Jesus does that.

You are left with a choice between two competing hypotheses arising from the evidence from NDEs and evidence from the gospels. You can choose to believe what the New Age faction of the NDE community who ignore negative NDEs, and indeed some Christians, declare—there is nothing to fear about death: we all make it. Or you can choose to believe what Jesus said, a position supported by evidence from NDEs: most will perish (90% of those who die and achieve ROSC do not have NDEs and therefore do not report going to heaven and up to 25% of NDEs are negative). According to Jesus only those who believe in him are assured eternal life in God's heaven. That choice is not dissimilar to the one described in Pascal's wager:

CHAPTER 9: PASCAL'S WAGER—WITH A TWIST

Pascal's wager is a philosophical argument advanced by Blaise Pascal (1623–1662), seventeenth-century French mathematician, philosopher, physicist, and theologian. This argument posits that individuals essentially engage in a life-defining gamble regarding the belief in the existence of God.

Pascal contends that a rational person should adopt a lifestyle consistent with the existence of God and actively strive to believe in God. The reasoning behind this stance lies in the potential outcomes: if God does not exist, the individual incurs only finite losses, potentially sacrificing certain pleasures and luxuries. However, if God does indeed exist, they stand to gain immeasurably, as represented for example by an eternity in Heaven in Abrahamic tradition, while simultaneously avoiding boundless losses associated with an eternity in Hell.[27]

In the context of all we have discussed, an adapted version of Pascal's wager is not a choice of belief in God versus atheism. We have proof beyond reasonable doubt that the soul survives death, there is a heaven, there is a God, and so on. Now, in the post-materialistic age I believe we may be about to enter, the choice is between believing in the NDE universalist position or in Jesus Christ's limited but inclusive declarations regarding the route to attaining eternal life and entry to heaven:

- You can choose to believe the universalist's assertion that everyone goes to heaven:
  - If you are right, then you are free to do whatever you want in this life and will go to heaven. You can party, become wildly wealthy, even rape, steal, murder, and lie as much as you like. You can engage in any religion, or none. You can ignore God and all the prophets He sent. It does not matter. As many NDErs claim, this life, or "earth school" as they are prone to calling it, is just about learning and ideally loving, there is no judgment at the end, but you may feel a bit bad about all the wrong you did when you do your life review. No matter, it was just a learning experience! The worst is you have to come back and do it all again.
  - If you are wrong, then your soul may be destroyed, possibly in hell.
- You can choose to believe the evidence that Jesus is God the Son, and that therefore His words are indeed the words of life:
  - If you are right, you are not free to behave exactly as you please in this life, but must make Him the Lord of your life, follow His teachings, and you may need to make significant sacrifices. Your reward will be to bypass the consequences of judgment and go straight to heaven for eternity.

- If you are wrong, and the universalists are right, *you will still go to heaven*, but you will have given up some pleasures and behaviors that are probably bad for you and others anyway, and maybe become less wealthy. In some circumstances, you may sacrifice more but, compared to eternal life, it is no sacrifice.

Given the stakes are so high—eternal and infinite, I think you will agree that the choice is a "no-brainer."

I will return to the "twist" at the very end, but first of all I want to grapple with one last question I promised I would deal with, the question of why we are given a choice. If God loves us, why does He not just create us in heaven or make things so utterly obvious that we all believe and are saved?

This is an important question, and it raises further related questions, such as, "Does God really love us and, if so, why? What are we to God? Where do our spirits come from?" To get the answer to that I need to deal with one further troublesome question, the one of whether a particular understanding of our existence, related to philosophical idealism, is correct. Let us deal with that first.

There is a view, which I have often encountered in those who are PhD scientists like me, and who have come to realize that the material world is not what it appears. This view holds that we are living either in a simulation or inside the mind of a great creator, either as a segmented part of that creator's consciousness or as a part of a created story. They believe that while we feel as though we are agents of free will, it is a lie, and that all our responses and behaviors are a function of predetermined characteristics built into us to create the illusion of free will. But ultimately, we are just characters within a giant story created to entertain a bored and lonely intelligent conscious being, whom we call God.

I get it. I accept why some could see that as a true interpretation of our existence. Ultimately, I have no objective evidence to disprove it, nor do they have evidence to prove it. It is all hypothetical conjecture. While I believe we have proof that this material world is not what it seems, my understanding of what it is is a result of my consciousness interpreting the information it is provided with. All my experiences could be fabricated to create the responses I have, and that my life and the lives of billions of others are indeed Netflix for this God. The illusion of choice, the inbuilt biases, and so on, create a degree of uncertainty in the outcome for each individual story that makes it compelling to watch.

I might have been tempted to go down this path but for my own experience of God which gives me faith that there is more to our existence than just being characters in someone else's entertainment. Now, some may say that very experience of God is in itself an illusion to help me maintain sufficient compliance to fulfil my part in this play. I cannot prove that to be wrong, I just believe it is wrong. At some point you have to choose what to believe.

I choose to believe that my experience of God and my understanding of our place in his creation, and his desires for us, are a true representation of "reality," and not part of a program designed to stop us from going crazy and ruining the story. This choice has its own element of Pascal's wager to it, although it is not quite so much of a win-win as the first one I just presented.

The wager:

- We can choose to be believe we are just the result of a simulation or entertainment for a bored "God" and there is not much we can do about it. One day he will press the remote and simply change channel and we are gone.
  - If we are right that choice will probably not make life better. We would likely spend our lives internally railing against the "Matrix," at best choosing to indulge in the illusory fleshly pleasures understanding that the consequences are of no consequence to us as individuals, because our sense of being an individual is an illusion.
  - If we are wrong, then we could be choosing a path that leads to a lost eternity, and spiritual destruction.
- On the other hand, we can choose to believe we are not in a simulation, but are independent souls with a free will, and to make the choice to believe in and follow Jesus:
  - if we are right, we bypass judgment and go to heaven;
  - if we are wrong, we may miss out on some "fun," but once the remote gets switched off, we will cease to exist anyway, so it is irrelevant.

In summary, we cannot know whether or not we are living in a simulation, but since we do have a choice, and given the outcomes from Pascal's wager, it is wiser to choose to believe we are not. You may have doubts to start with, but the further you go down that road, the smaller the doubts become, until they have receded so far into the distance because of the certainty of the experiences you have in God, they disappear. That, at least, is my experience.

So, if we, as in our consciousness, are not a figment of God's imagination, or the product of a computer simulation, what are we?

I believe God has provided an analogue in this life to help us understand where we come from, and He uses that analogue in the revelations He gives us.

We are His children. We are somehow birthed from His own consciousness, His own soul, His own spirit, just as children are birthed from us.

Children would not exist without the will of their parents (ideally). Children are entirely composed of material that came from the parents—they came out of the parents, and yet while they may have certain characteristics of their parents, they are different from them—they are independent, sentient beings. While some parents try to live vicariously through their children, or to control them, ultimately children have independent choice from their parents and their existence is entirely their own to make of what they wish.

So it is with God. Somehow, our consciousness, or spirit, has come out of God, and while we have some characteristics of God (we are made in His image), we are unique, independent and given free choice. This is how I meet the challenge of the idea that we are just a part of His imagination. This is how I can understand and accept my existence in the face of existential questions.

Let us extend the analogue and at the same time allow some (or even a lot of) creative or speculative license. Just like when parents choose to have children, they are taking a risk. I have seen good parents produce both angels and monsters. Same upbringing, same parents, yet one will be good the other bad, Cain and Abel being a great example. So also, I believe is the case with God. Despite His being entirely good, when He "births" souls and gives them choice, they can choose good and evil. They can choose Him or choose another way. Christians may say God cannot create evil, but many understand evil just to be a lack of good, or a lack of God, just as darkness is a lack of light, or cold a lack of warmth, Hell a place with no goodness.

Whatever you think about angels and demons, if you believe NDEs to be true, then angels seem to exist. Many Christians in this life claim to have experience of both angels and demons. It is likely we all do without realizing it. What little we know about these beings from the Bible is that they too are spiritual beings that came out of God, and who also were given free will. However, some of these beings did in fact exist in God's heaven. Despite the perfection of God's heaven, and the glory of being in His presence, it appears that some angels, led by a chap called Lucifer, or Satan, rebelled. All they had experienced was good, but it was not enough for them—they wanted control, independence outside of God's will, which pervades throughout all of heaven. Their rebellion probably caused quite the stink in the celestial realm, and just like human children can present a threat to the order of a home, so too can spiritual children. Despite His love for them, their presence could no longer be tolerated, and God booted them out, and apparently sent them to this earthly realm.

Extending the creative, or imaginative, license further, after recovering from this rebellion and the implications of it, God decided enough with the children being born in heaven, let us allow these children to be born into a safe test environment so we do not get indigestion after arguments over Sunday lunch. If they turn out to be bad eggs, then they will be destroyed through their own choices, but if they are good, we will welcome them into our heaven. To ensure we were properly tested, He birthed us in the very place He sent all the rebels and allowed them to influence us. If we manage to find God and choose Him despite all the lies and temptations the enemies of God put in our way, then we are good enough to be with Him. If not, we get to stay with them and be destroyed.

Unfortunately, the enemies of God are very good at what they do, resulting in humans often choosing the ways of God's enemies. So, God decided to give humanity one last chance, and appeared Himself in the form of Jesus, spelt it out as clearly as He could, without removing free will, and let things progress from there.

For 1,800 years the message of Christ spread to all parts of the world, and nearly everyone was given the choice to believe, and it felt like a choice. However, in recent centuries, following the discoveries of Darwin, it has felt harder to make that choice. The balance of evidence appeared to favor the idea that God never existed. However, the pendulum has been swinging the other way ever since Hubble disproved Einstein and the scientific consensus of the early twentieth century, that the universe was static. Out of Hubble's ideas were born the Big Bang theory and the understanding the universe is expanding and therefore had a beginning, which brought huge philosophical challenges with it. Then, in the 1960s, with the discovery of DNA and the subsequent elucidation of the genetic code and how it was translated, it became blindingly obvious that life could not have come into existence by unguided natural means.

Now, with the proof of the consciousness being able to survive death we have come full circle to where we were before Darwin. However, the West has abandoned its Christian roots. But we still clearly have a choice.

God births billions of souls and loves each of them wildly. Just like any parent, He longs for them to love Him back. However, just as when a rich parent does not know if their child loves them because of who they are or because they want to inherit their wealth, so too if God made His existence obvious, and faith in Him so obviously compelling in order to attain the unimaginable riches of eternity in His heaven, He would not know if our love for Him was real, or rather we would all have no choice but to love Him. So, He came as a humble man, born in humble circumstances, in a backwater of the Roman Empire, and revealed Himself to a select few from equally humble origins. He did not do it in a time where His miracles would have been recorded on film, as that would have removed choice. That is one of the reasons why I believe we do not see many miracles that often now. The evidence would compel people to believe and remove choice. Jesus described much of the reality we have been discussing here, but in parables, or riddles.

For instance, the parable of the sower. The sower is God, and the seeds are the souls He births. Just like any farmer would want every seed to germinate, take root, and grow into a strong healthy plant, so too does God want us to grow and be healthy, but not all do.

Satan asks Jesus if He can "sift" the disciples (Luke 22:31). This sifting is testing. The testing is temptation. Wheat that is no good will be destroyed. That which is good will be kept, made into bread, and put in an oven, then gobbled—OK, maybe best not to extend the analogy too far!

Anyway, whatever the specifics of everything, this place where we find ourselves, this created dimension where we exist, is a testing environment in which our souls are tested for goodness. Even if we have done bad things, those who are truly good will in themselves recognize Jesus for who He is and accept His offer.

This is a key distinction between NDEism and Christianity. NDEism claims earth is a school; Christianity tells us it is a test. If we fail the test, our souls will die or be destroyed. Jesus says this. He says, if we follow Him, we will not die but have eternal life.

This, I believe, is the truth about our existence. This choice is the be all and end all of our existence.

If you have not already chosen, or you know someone who has not chosen but is genuinely curious and seeking answers, then I believe the evidence I have presented in this book provides as much as you are ever going to get that points the way. But despite the evidence (I have selected due to my bias) supporting this position, if you are a universalist like Parnia, it is possible to construct an argument for universalism by selecting evidence that supports your bias. I really believe the evidence I have is stronger, but so too do universalists regarding their evidence! But, and of existential importance, only one position can be right. There is a choice. Let us return to Pascal's wager.

As I showed at the beginning of this chapter, the choice is a bit of a no-brainer.

Why?

If you choose to believe that everyone will make it to heaven, and that there is no need to do anything in this life to attain eternal life, but you are wrong, you may lose an eternal future, and possibly worse. However, if you choose to believe in Jesus, then if you are right, you go to heaven. But even if you are wrong, and the universalists are right, while you made some sacrifices in this life, you will still get to go to heaven! Truly a win-win situation!

Now for the twist.

In fact, Pascal does hint at this. You must really believe. There is no room for half-heartedness. You cannot hoodwink God. As Jesus says, there will be many who have called Him Lord who will be turned away as they did not believe actively.

From personal experience I can tell you that the more you let faith lead you—and faith consists of blind steps you take in trust without knowing where your foot lands—the less it becomes about faith and the easier it becomes to believe with all your heart soul, and mind, and act accordingly. With each blind step you take, and then find your toes being tickled by lush green grass covering firm ground, the readier you are to take the next blind step. The more you give of yourself to God through faith in Jesus, the more of Himself and His vast and endless love He reveals to you. I, and many others, having traveled a long way down this path, have learned that this being is not only real and living among us in His spirit form, but is completely trustworthy and that Jesus is this same trustworthy being who walked among us in human form. I believe His promise that I will one day stand before His ultimate, unveiled form in His heaven and experience that cascade of love I felt as a teen once again. However, you can reach that point only by taking your first step of faith.

If you have not already done so, then, I promise you, there is nothing to lose and everything to gain by taking that first step toward Jesus. Say the sinner's prayer (below) out loud, and then tell someone you did it and find a church where God is truly present so you can worship Him, join His family and learn His ways. If you did that in the past, but know you have not believed with your actions, then repeat the prayer and recommit yourself to active faith. You will never completely succeed, but if you never give up, you will get closer to achieving that ultimate goal of being in the "likeness of Jesus."

Lord Jesus, I have sinned, I have done wrong, I have ignored you and disobeyed you,

I am truly sorry, please forgive me for all my wrongdoings.

I acknowledge that you are God the Son, the Lord of heaven and I make you my Lord.

Please, I beg, through your Holy Spirit here on earth, come into my life, help me to repent, help me to leave behind my life of wrongdoing, help me to become like you. Amen.

APPENDIX

MEMORY WHEN THERE IS NO BRAIN

NDErs' claims of having memory poses an interesting question: How can they remember if their brains are not functioning, as proven by flatlining EEG? In other words, how can a completely shut-down brain lay down memory?

This opens up Pandora's box, so to speak. It has been assumed that memories are stored in the brain through the connection of neurons. If memories are stored somewhere other than the brain, where else are they stored? The answer to this may lie in two other aspects of NDEs that have been reported over the years.

First, people who report having a "life review" during an NDE report experiencing all the events of their life, and not just from their own perspective but from the perspective of those around them and those affected by their behavior. If a person's memories were stored only in his or her brain, this viewing from multiple perspectives would not be possible since these memories would only be accessible in the individuals brain and then die with the brain when the person dies.

Second, some NDErs reported witnessing historical events they were not even present at, from the perspective of participants in those events. Again, this would not be possible if the participants' memories of their existence were stored only in their individual brains. This perhaps suggests that all experience is stored "centrally" in some giant spiritual server—a library of all experience—and access is granted to anyone who has "passed over" to that dimension. In our modern times, we know that artificial memory can be stored electronically in computers, and that if you have the right computer and a good Internet connection, you can access that memory from anywhere else in the world. In a dimension beyond our understanding, is it not therefore conceivable that all events could somehow be recorded in an analogous way?

I find this incredibly exciting, as I mentioned earlier. I love history and find it fascinating, and to know that I may be able to witness all human history—and maybe some non-human is extremely exciting.

ENDNOTES

NOTES AND REFERENCES

1—The Story of God with Morgan Freeman, produced by the National Geographic Channel and released in April 2016. Now available on Netflix.

2   Parnia, S, et al. Guidelines and standards for the study of death and recalled experiences of death—a multidisciplinary consensus statement and proposed future directions. *Annals of the New York Academy of Sciences*. May 2022. Vol 1511(1): p5–21.

3   Vrselja, Z, Daniele, SG, Silbereis, J, et al. Restoration of brain circulation and cellular functions hours post-mortem. *Nature*. 2019. Vol 568: p336–343.

4   Wanscher, M, et al. Outcome of accidental hypothermia with or without circulatory arrest—experience from the Danish Præstø Fjord boating accident. *Resuscitation*. Vol 83(9): p1078–1084.

5   Gilbert, M, Busund, R, Skagseth, A, Nilsen, P, Solbo, J. Resuscitation from accidental hypothermia of 13.7°C with circulatory arrest. *The Lancet*. 2000. Vol 355(Issue 9201): p375–376.

6   *Canadian Family Physician*. July 2018. Vol 64(7): p514–517.

7   Van Lommel, P. Near-death experience in survivors of cardiac arrest: a prospective study in the Netherlands. *The Lancet* 2001. Vol 358: p2039–2045.

8   Greyson, B. Incidence and correlates of near-death experiences in a cardiac care unit. *General Hospital Psychiatry*. July–Aug 2003. Vol 25(4): p269–276.

9   Parnia, S, Waller DG, Yeates, R, Fenwick, P. A qualitative and quantitative study of the incidence, features and etiology of near-death experiences in cardiac arrest survivors. *Resuscitation*. Feb 2001. Vol 48(2): p149–156.

10 Parnia, S, et al. AWARE—AWAreness during REsuscitation—a prospective study. *Resuscitation*. Dec 2014. Vol 85 (12): p1799–1805.

11 Parnia, S, et al. AWAreness during REsuscitation—II: a multi-center study of consciousness and awareness in cardiac arrest. *Resuscitation*, July 2023. Vol 191.: p109903.

12 Beauregard, M. Conscious mental activity during a deep hypothermic cardiocirculatory arrest? Resuscitation Vol 83(1): E19

13 Borjigin, J, Lee, U, Liu, T, et al. Surge of neurophysiological coherence and connectivity in the dying brain. *Proceedings of the National Academy of Science*. 2013. Vol 110(35): p14432–14437.

14 Borjigin, J, et al. Surge of neurophysiological coupling and connectivity of gamma oscillations in the dying human brain. *Proceedings of the National Academy of Science*. May 2023. Vol 120(19): p14432.

15 Cassol, H, et al. A systematic analysis of distressing near-death experience accounts; https://doi.org/10.1080/09658211.2019.1626438.

16 Article in Christian Scholars Review by Michael Zigarelli https://christianscholars.com/near-death-experiences-and-the-emerging-implications-for-christian-theology/

17 The figure of 85% is cited by the International Association of Near Death Studies (IANDS). Morse, M, added further evidence in a later book, *Parting Visions: A New Scientific Paradigm*. In Bailey, LW, Yates, J, eds. The near-death experience: a reader. New York and London: Routledge, 1996: p299–318.

18 PsychCorp. Wechsler Memory Scale-Fourth Edition (WMS-IV) Technical and Interpretative Manual. San Antonio, TX, Pearson, 2009.

19   Trelle, AN. Episodic memory decline in healthy ageing. Department of Psychology, St John's College. Dissertation for the degree of Doctor of Philosophy. University of Cambridge. May 2016.

20   Levine, B, Svoboda, E, Hay, J, Winocur, G, & Moscovitch, M. Aging and autobiographical memory: dissociating episodic from semantic retrieval. *Psychology and Aging*. 2002. Vol 17, p677–689.

21   Craik, FIM. Memory changes in normal aging. *Current Directions in Psychological Science*. 1994. Vol 3, p155–158.

22   Schacter, Koutstaal, & Norman. False memories and aging. *Trends in Cognitive Sciences*. 1997. Vol 1, p229–236.

23   Koen and Yonelinas. *Neuropsychology Review*. Sept 2014. Vol 24(3): p332–354.

24   Nielson, T. Variations in dream recall frequency and dream theme diversity by age and sex. *Frontiers in Neurology*. 2012. Vol 3: p106.

25   Van Lommel, P. Near-death experience in survivors of cardiac arrest: a prospective study in the Netherlands. *Lancet*. 2001. Vol 358: p2039–2045.

26   https://neo.life/2022/08/your-brain-at-the-moment-of-death.

27   https://en.wikipedia.org/wiki/Pascal%27s_wager

MY THANKS AND A SMALL REQUEST

Dear Reader,

I hope you enjoyed *Did Jesus Die For Nothing*. Please remember to rate and/or review on whichever site you purchased it from, and to let your friends and associates know about it.

Thanks!

All the very best,

Orson

BY THE SAME AUTHOR

Other books by Orson Wedgwood available on Amazon and other e-retailers in physical and e-book formats:

Fiction

Deadly Medicine

Unholy Spirit: Part 1

Non-Fiction

DNA: The Elephant In The Lab

NDE and the AWARE studies: Proof Of The Soul and God

ACKNOWLEDGEMENTS

I would like to thank Lisa Stilwell and Eldo Barkhuizen for their excellent editing skills and theological comments to ensure this book is as linguistically and biblically correct as possible. In addition, I would like to thank Mark Thomas who I have worked with on a number of projects now for his excellent cover and interior design work. Finally, and most all, I would like to thank my amazing wife, Kirsty Wedgwood, for her endless support, encouragement, editorial input and sense checking.

ABOUT THE AUTHOR

Born in London and now living in Sussex, England, with his wife Kirsty, Orson has spent his career in science and communicating science. His undergraduate studies were in chemistry, and his PhD studies were in organic medicinal chemistry, during which he worked in a team that created a molecule that opened the door to a cure for Hepatitis C, as well as treatments for certain cancers, and HIV. Since attaining his doctorate, he has worked as a medical scientist communicating science as well as writing fiction and nonfiction books.

Orson writes a blog—awareofaware.com—exploring research into NDEs, which follows closely any developments in the NDE studies. The blog focuses on the clinical data and the science. He also discusses possible "spiritual" implications that come out of the scientific research.

For more information about Orson and his writing, please visit **orsonw.com**

www.ingramcontent.com/pod-product-compliance
Lightning Source LLC
Chambersburg PA
CBHW072052110526
44590CB00018B/3139